LANCET

CW01011202

TM282 OU JOINT

SCHOOL 1989

THE NEW MANAGER

Mike Woods works in the Post Experience Programmes of Bradford University Management Centre, developing and teaching in programmes for working managers. Companies with whom he is currently engaged include BP, Shell, GKN, Elida Gibbs . . . He specialises in working with recently appointed managers who need to develop the new skills of people management and programmes on Assertive Behaviour and Change Management.

He is training associate of Leeds University Psychology Department CCDU, where he is involved with helping teachers to adjust to the current major changes taking place in British education. He is also an adviser on change for a major UK charity, and has worked with the DHSS on a similar project. He has appeared in and worked on several television programmes on Assertive Behaviour and is now preparing two books on the subject for Element. He is married with a large family of varying ages and enjoys talking, walking and dogs.

THE NEW MANAGER

A GUIDE TO IMPROVING THE SKILLS

OF PEOPLE MANAGEMENT

FOR NEWLY APPOINTED MANAGERS

Mike Woods

ELEMENT BOOKS

© Dr. Mike Woods 1988

First published 1988 by
Element Books Limited
Longmead, Shaftesbury, Dorset

Printed and bound in Great Britain by Billings, Hylton Road, Worcester

Designed by Max Fairbrother

Cover illustration by Peter Till

British Library Cataloguing in Publication Data
Woods, Mike
    The new manager.
    1. Management
    I. Title
    658.4

ISBN 1-85230-036-1

CONTENTS

ACKNOWLEDGEMENTS

The New Manager covers what is known in my trade as 'management psychology'. As this book has been written for busy people we do not intend to provide an academically worthy bibliography, merely, and in our view more usefully, a guide to further reading.

Chapter 3
Born to Win, Muriel James and Dorothy Jungewald (Addison Wesley, 1971) - a guide to the ideas and concepts of Eric Berne.

Chapter 4
The One Minute Manager, Kenneth Blanchard and Spencer Johnson (Fontana, Collins, 1983)

Chapter 7
Management Teams, R. Meredith Belbin (Heinemann, 1981)

Chapter 8
The Disorganised Manager, (Video Arts Training Film, London)
Experiential Learning, D.A. Kolb (Prentice Hall, 1986)
The Rational Manager, Kepner and Tregoe (Mc Graw Hill, 1965)

Chapter 10
In Search of Excellence, Tom Peters and Robert H. Waterman (Harper & Row, 1982)

Quotations are gratefully acknowledged from:
' The Unknown Citizen ', *Selected poems W. H. Auden* (Faber & Faber, 1979)
' The General Motors poem ', *In Search of Excellence* (Harper & Row, 1982)
and from my many friends who have inadvertently acted as resources for this book.

AUTHOR'S NOTE

The book is written by a working trainer and as such will contain material from many sources. The principal sources are acknowledged and include Berne, Peters and Waterman, Kepner and Tregoe, Kolb, and Belbin. There will also be, unavoidably, material culled and developed from the work of other trainers, notably the two Mikes – Fordham and Carpenter – Beryl Heather and generically from the Career Counselling and Development Unit of Leeds University Psychology Department. If you recognise more of your ideas than you think fit, please let us know so that we may acknowledge your contribution in later editions. In the meantime, I, Mike Woods on behalf of the Element Books team, apologise.

Even more seriously, I have included throughout this book certain Case Studies. No Case Study is founded on one single incident, company or individual. Each and every Case Study is a composite designed to press a point in a factual way. If, as a manager, you think you recognise yourself or your organisation in a favourable light – please accept our good wishes. If, however, you think you recognise yourself or your organisation presented unfavourably, please be reconciled by the fact that your issue has been made much worse by including problems from a person or organisation with more intractable problems than yourself.

PREFACE

This book is dedicated to those who were happy doing the job they knew but have suddenly found out that they now have to get others to do it for them. From being specialists they have moved, by force of circumstance or ambition, to being managers. They may have enjoyed being effective door-step social workers, but now they have to manage other social workers – they have been given a department or even a region to run. They may have been technical specialists writing computer codes, but now they are being asked to control a team of specialists writing code or even building the computers themselves. They may have been skilled craftsmen on the shop floor and been recognised for 'management potential', but all of them – social worker, computer specialist or craftsman – will now share similar problems. *Management is the direction of resources, including people, towards a goal; whereas before, their skills lay in working with resources, including people, towards a goal.* This new form of words in the New Manager's job definition is responsible for presenting a new challenge that will involve every aspect of his or her personality. As the door-step social worker, computer specialist or skilled craftsman, the rewards may have come from the demonstration of a hard-won skill. Others will now get those rewards, and the new skills of management may be slow in coming and only recognised in their absence. The rewards may have come partly from community, but as a manager directing people, he or she may be forced into isolation.

The skills of management are concerned with the *process* of work and not with the *task* itself. New Managers who succeed may well have to learn about budgets and unions, markets and planning, but mostly the learning will need to be about themselves and other people. This book is designed to help this journey.

CHAPTER ONE

→

Beginning the Journey

I HAVE MADE MANY TRANSITIONS in my own life – from practising bench chemist to commissioning engineer, from active engineer to adviser on new processes and products, and then to manager of a team producing its own projects. From then I managed a training centre, became interested in the task of training itself and gratefully accepted that others could prefer management to the job of being an actual trainer. For me, training, working with 'real' managers and helping them with real issues, is now part of my life and provides me with rich personal rewards.

By far the most difficult transition for me was from worker and adviser to manager. I liked the clarity of a 'real job' and the challenge it presented to me, and resented the blurred boundaries I found when I had to 'direct resources and people towards a goal'.

Having moved towards introducing myself as your author and your tutor, how do I, the producer of this book, see you? Well, I see you as a very busy person who has potential access to a huge volume of books and courses on management. The advice is available and I can almost hear you saying:

'I already know how to be twice as good a manager as I will ever be.'

or perhaps:

'Yes . . . but you don't know how it is for me.'

You are correct – I 'don't know how it is' exactly, but I can get very near the truth. And I suspect that you have found very little of the available advice relevant to your actual job once the euphoria has settled.

I also see you at a major transition point in your working life, with similarities to my own move from process and product developer to departmental manager. For me, and I suspect you, all my formal training up to the transition from worker to manager had been directed towards creating an effective chemist and engineer who did tangible things. I derived great satisfaction from being good at the job and thinking I did it better than the next engineer. I then found that to progress I had to become a manager. I had to search for new skills, to flex muscles in my personality that had had no previous work experience. I see you at the same transition. Your own skills were devoted to performing some task, and most probably you derived great satisfaction from performing that task well. You may have been a social worker called upon to manage a department, or you may have been a draughtsman called upon to control a floor of draughtsmen and machines. Whatever you *were*, now you need to get others to perform tasks within an organisation.

Although some of you may own the organisation within which you now find yourself a manager, I see this as the exception. Most of us will work in organisations which existed before and will exist after our stint is ended. We are mostly cogs within mysterious machines and to function effectively we need to know something of the machine and for what purpose our cog is intended. Unfortunately, much of our stress is caused by not having either bit of this information.

In your new-found managerial posts I see you attempting to behave rationally, intelligently and responsibly, but somehow those around you seem to reserve the right to behave as the mood takes them. Sometimes you allow yourself to be charitable over the inconsistencies coming from your bosses, peers and subordinates, but on bad days you feel that their behaviour amounts almost to a deliberate sabotage of your efforts. You expected your new job to have some logic, but you find it like some chess game with variable rules, changing pieces and the occasional incident that knocks the table over. The changes in the way that you are judged may be so rapid that the temptation is to become purely reactive, and you see other managers around you gently but inexorably being defeated as they attempt to run up the downstaircase of their careers.

This book is designed to allow you to face the problems that are so apparent and remain proactive: it is structured in such a way as to allow you to identify the particular issues that are important to you. Each chapter contains a series of exercises, and the subsequent pages will attempt to begin you on the journey of understanding and developing your own solutions. The exercises would best be done in small groups, and you may like to bring in your peers and perhaps even your family. If involving other people is impossible, a compromise would be to jot down notes before turning over the pages.

The book is not designed to give solutions. Your job is unique and is shaped by your own strengths and weaknesses, its purpose and its constraints. The only person who can make you more effective is yourself. Let's try the first exercise.

————————▶

EXERCISE

As a New Manager and understanding something of what is required of you in your new opportunity:

What Blocks and Barriers do you see that could prevent you being more effective?

Write down about twenty personal statements. Examples could include:

1. I don't really understand accounts.
2. I keep getting into pointless rows.
3. I dislike Mr Bloggs, the Operations Director.
4. I am not very good on committees.
5. I have a beard.
6. . . .

Look at your list and decide which of the twenty you would be happy to see becoming public knowledge, which you would prefer to have a limited circulation and which you would prefer to remain hidden except in very special circumstances. Make this classification from the standpoint of your old job as a 'worker' and of your new job as a manager.

Is there any pattern when you compare the two lists?

————————▶

The lists you have begun will provide your own personal agenda for reading and working with this book, so please do not lose them. We will use the lists in several ways, but first let's see how your views of what it was wise to have disclosed differed before and after the transition from 'worker' to manager. In the list I quoted as an example, I suspect that 'having a beard', if true, could be common knowledge and that both as a worker and as a manager the lack of understanding of accounts is a training need (should such understanding be essential to the job). We would not

splash the deficiency about and in either role we might be careful
to whom we confided the information, but there the matter rests.
On our effectiveness on committees we may well find that greater
care needs to be exercised about disclosure as a manager than as a
worker. What might be a joke on the bench may well be a matter
for careful delegation and private counselling in the managerial
post. The same might be said of the tendency to get into pointless
rows. At least the issue has been acknowledged and you are
reading the correct book to tackle the problem, but how about our
issue with Mr Bloggs? Mr Bloggs is our boss and, as a worker, not
getting on with the boss is a fact of life. We are only working *with*
our colleagues. As a manager we represent *all* management, and
having a personal animosity to Mr Bloggs, a Senior Manager, is
something that is a major issue in such representation. Disliking
Mr Bloggs may well need to be a 'hidden area' as a manager,
whereas 'limited circulation' is probably all right for the worker.

The fact that the information in the three classifications of
Open, Limited Circulation and Hidden is different in the old and
new job lists presents the first problem that I find universal to the
newly promoted manager. The discrepancy is worst when the
promotion is direct – a shop-floor worker is promoted overnight
to some form of manager or supervisor – and can be ameliorated
by degrees of separation as the transition takes place. Many
companies send candidates for senior promotions on long training
programmes to emphasise the transition, but it does not always
happen and I find it rarely happens on junior appointments.

The New Manager needs to have a strategy ready for remarks
like:

'You never did that when you were doing the job.'

'You know that won't work here.'

'You tell them – you know how it is.'

'That's not like you at all.'

or perhaps not too humorously:

'You wait till my wife tells your Doris.'

Imagine your work-relevant personality as a room with a window
to the outside world. The window has three sections, the first of
which is composed of completely clear glass. Everything in your
'room' behind this clear glass is completely open to the outside
world. The second section of the window has shutters which can
be opened by you in certain circumstances to allow a select band of
people to see in. The third section of your window is of blackened
glass and what happens behind has been chosen by you to remain
hidden.

I am saying that, by design or circumstance, the amounts of your personality behind the clear glass, the shutters and the blackened section adjust to any role you may have. When the role changes, for your own survival the ratio of clarities in the window needs to change as well. I am also saying that the transition from managed to manager involves the most significant readjustment of all and that it is this readjustment that causes you, the New Manager, most grief.

A New Manager starting with a new group of staff, colleagues and bosses faces a different problem from one who has been promoted through the ranks. The New Manager starting afresh can ideally choose how much he or she wishes to have as common knowledge, what to keep in appropriate and limited circulation and what should remain hidden. If the choice is wise, then the manager can begin to take the middle- and long-term views of the job that are the hallmarks of good management. The good manager is able to rise out of the immediate fire-fighting involvement and look down. It is as if the good manager has a helicopter from which it is possible to rise out of the immediate scene and look at the plains beyond. The medium- and long-term views may well mean that the manager is not able to work for the short-term good of the group or individuals. If people know you too well, then this dis-involvement is doubly difficult. The New Manager's helicopter is stuck in the mud and is unable to take off.

Let's move on, towards your strengths and weaknesses. Why do you think you got promoted and what is required of you now?

----------▶

EXERCISE

Think of yourself before promotion to the managerial role. What did you see as your strengths and weaknesses as seen by you, your peers and your boss?

Now think of yourself in the New Manager role and look back at your list of Blocks and Barriers. What now do you see as your strengths and weaknesses and what knowledge, skills and aptitudes do you think you need to acquire to improve on your strengths and reduce your weaknesses?

----------▶

Suppose we look at your list of strengths and weaknesses first. We will assume that moving into a managerial role involves promotion and that somebody else needed to be convinced that you deserved that promotion. What did *they* see as your qualities:

Sound at the job, knows it now and is happy to learn
Respected by colleagues, reliable
Seems to be able to see the reason for doing things
The person you naturally go to in the section
The best person to sort the problem out
Is management potential and should go far

These outsiders that are so important in our lives are also very aware of the risks of promotion, and the risks are expressed in the single word 'potential'. Management is always an ordeal by fire, and the difference between a good manager and a disaster is about handling the new and the different. The outsiders realise that you will need new or revised knowledge and skills for the job and are probably willing to back you as having the correct aptitudes for acquiring them. You may well know better. When you review your own strengths for the job, think of them in terms of the concepts that *they* saw in you. Look at the last two concepts – 'The best person to sort the problem out' and 'Management potential and should go far'. In the first you are still seen as a 'worker' with specialist skills, in the second you are seen not as a competent worker but as a present and future leader. If the latter is so, then you need to discard and delegate all your 'worker' skills and aptitudes, for these are no longer what you are to be judged upon. The problem solver may wish to prove his or her managerial skills in the new-found opportunity, but he or she will be judged by the completion of the task: the rest is a bonus. The 'worker with potential' is in a higher risk and higher opportunity game with no return ticket.

With such an insight it is possible to review what knowledge, skills and aptitudes you need to be effective. Have a look at your list and see whether the items on it help to bring together your needs for survival and growth, your ambitions, the way you judge yourself and the way others will judge you.

---------->

EXERCISE

Case Study 1

John worked in a bank and was recognised for having a particular nose for irregularities. His manager respected his advice when business clients required loans, and his looking beyond the balance sheet had proved invaluable. The bank decided to form a new department to integrate Government and bank policy for small business loans, and John was recommended as section manager within that department concerned with primary screening.

Case Study 2

Mary is married to a sales manager of a multinational and has returned to work after a ten-year break to have a family. Her degree was in Economics but on her return to work she took a job in personnel in the local branch of a nationwide retailing group. Not much was expected of her at first, but at the insistence of her boss her training plans for the local supermarket staff were sent to Head Office. In only slightly revised form, these plans were adopted nationally and Mary was asked to accept a junior management post in Head Office to oversee implementation.

Look at the two case studies in terms of the strengths and weaknesses of both John and Mary as perceived by themselves and by their managers. Both are being given New Manager roles, but the difference lies behind what is expected of them in these roles. What Knowledge, Skills and Aptitudes do John and Mary need to concentrate on acquiring, and what are the particular Blocks and Barriers against being effective they are likely to meet?

Although both examples are of specialists becoming New Managers, there is a world of difference between the worlds of John and Mary. Both are being given a great opportunity to do something new, to achieve in management a capability they have demonstrated on an individual scale: John could 'smell' discrepancies and now he has to manage a department that 'smells' discrepancies; Mary could train her own store staff effectively and now she has to manage the staff training of the group. The differences lie in what is expected of both of them.

John will be judged on the completion of a particular task, the setting up of a 'system'. For this he will certainly have to acquire an increased knowledge of bank and Government policies, but he will be working with skilled staff and the strategic implications will not be in his hands. He may need to work on presentation skills and perhaps one-to-one communication but, unless something terrible happens, he has the aptitude. If John makes a success, he may well be able to choose between another Head Office staff or management job or a branch of the bank to run as manager when one turns up.

Mary is in a different position. She could do the job allocated standing on her head. She may need a 'top up' of skills and she will need a strong briefing on the 'who is who' in the organisation, but she and her bosses know the job will be done. Her bosses are looking at the way she does the job: her trial is about her potential in the company. Mary is concerned with aptitude – and only she knows what she wants, her own self-doubts and what she will sacrifice.

I would now like you to look at the blocks and barriers that could hold you back from being more effective. For instance if we had asked John and Mary to write down their blocks and barriers, John's might include:

1. I have great difficulty understanding Government policy statements.
2. I find it difficult to stop doing everything myself.
3. I lose my temper when people stall.
4. . . .

and Mary might write:

1. I simply don't have time to do all that needs to be done and still have a private life.
2. I find myself continually fire-fighting.
3. Things happen in the organisation that I am not privy to and I don't seem to be heading in the direction I want to go.
4. . . .

Over the years, and as a result of asking hundreds of managers to complete a similar exercise, I have come across hundreds of different blocks and barriers. This book is structured round a classification of the issues raised. Each chapter will begin with a simple list of the typical issues it attempts to tackle, and the reader may like to look at my classification as a way of guiding him or her most efficiently through the book. You may also learn something about the culture of the company or organisations within which you work by looking at your lists. Effective and secure people working in effective and secure organisations will be looking for growth in their lists. They will want to do the job better. Managers in less effective organisations may well be looking for personal survival and little more.

I would like you to look at your lists and if possible share them with other managers with whom you have rapport. But before you do this, look at your own list. This will contain three categories of blocks and barriers:

The need for new or improved *knowledge*
The need for new or improved *skills*
The need for different *aptitudes*

The blocks and barriers to improved effectiveness could mean that you need increased knowledge of financial method, you need new skills with computers, and basically you find the conflicts that are part of the job difficult to handle as a person.

You have the power to look at the lists and see whether you want to find a solution. Ted Matchett, an early guru in management philosophy, classified barriers in a completely different way:

Can I ignore them?
Can I climb over them?
Can I fight them?

I would add the final point – *Do I want to?*

We are not going to ask you to ignore personal factors: these are likely to be the very things that you as a New Manager need to tackle. You may find yourself getting into pointless rows and lacking assertiveness with senior management. You may also find that you have issues with individuals and that sharing your blocks and barriers with your peers helps you see these problems in perspective. The management aphorism that 'if a manager has no problems then *he* is the problem' may sober some of you.

I have chosen to structure the book around the problem statements I have received from the hundreds of managers I have met and have set the same exercise as you. The second chapter is concerned with communication at its most basic and is called 'Knowing Yourself'. It tackles such problem statements as:

'I never seem to be able to judge the effect my words have on other people.'

'If I can see people it's OK, but when I have to use the telephone or – worse still – write, then the trouble starts.'

'There is never any time to plan; things just seem to happen and I have to react.'

'I know that I intend to act as a model of probity, but others seem to see me as some kind of monster.'

'Somebody always takes my written memos the wrong way.'

The third chapter is also concerned with communications, but seeks to develop a language to help us understand and cope with more difficult issues as expressed by such problem statements as:

'I find myself getting into pointless rows.'

'I try to be consistent when I give instructions. Sometimes they do what I say, sometimes they get angry, and sometimes I can see that they are just waiting for me to be out of the way.'

'My boss tries to be nice all the time and everyone gets hurt.'

'My problem is giving instructions to different people; I just do not judge the best way.'

'I can hear people say, "Well if that's how you feel you'd better do it yourself".'

and we carry over one problem statement from Chapter 2 with new insights:

'If I can see people it's OK, but when I have to use the telephone or – worse still – write, then the trouble starts.'

However, we start Chapter 3 with an issue near to any trainer's heart:

'Psychology might be able to help me if wasn't for that terrible jargon.'

For that is what Chapter 3 is really about – a language with which to understand human behaviour.

Chapter 4 is concerned with the basic issues of staff motivation from the viewpoint of a New Manager who is unlikely to be able to control the purse strings of his or her organisation. The first problem statement almost says it all:

'How do I motivate staff – I can't hire, fire, discipline, or even control rewards.'

And I understand. What is said is certainly true, and to be useful this book has to tackle this problem along with the others:

'Our company provides sports facilities, medicare, pensions, the lot. It may get better people at interviews, but it certainly doesn't motivate existing people; they take it all for granted.'

'My people have to do boring jobs – someone has to. They get bored.'

'The company does its best to make people belong, but who wants a gold watch these days?'

Whereas Chapter 4 deals with people in general, as a mass, Chapter 5 helps us to understand that different people need motivating in different ways, and also begins to deal with the relationship between the demands of work and the demands of our home life. It tackles such issues as:

'When I get home I just want to get a beer, put my feet up and watch the telly – anything. My wife wants to talk; I could kill her.'

'With promotion I just don't get any real time with the family.'

'I used to like the company get-togethers; now I find them embarrassing.'

'If only I could delegate more.'

'I do all this "hello" stuff to my staff, but some people seem to want it all the time.'

'I like people and especially my group, so when I give difficult orders and they turn their backs, I feel bad.'

The consequences of what can be roughly described as 'why people work', on their performance in teams are the subject of Chapter 6. I recognise that teams mature and that the behaviour of an immature team calls for different management skills from that of a fully operational team:

'How the hell do you get them down to work in the morning? They just seem to want to natter.'

'I need to get on with the job, but so much seems to be going on they don't hear me.'

'This organisation . . . it's all covering up for mistakes, blame and recriminations.'

We are beginning to talk about management as a role, and the discussion moves into Chapter 7. Managers differ and the composition of teams is not always ideal:

'My style of management seems to be different – am I wrong?'

'I finish doing *everything*.'

'I find myself saying, "Get out of the way, I'll do it myself".'

'I always seem to be stepping on my boss's toes.'

'The team should be OK: it's got all the right skills, but it doesn't function properly – rows and unfinished work.'

Chapter 8 takes on the issues of the functions of a manager. I shall discuss perceptions of management and the problems when perceptions differ:

'I'm told to set objectives . . . how?'

'I see my job as a sort of facilitator, but my boss doesn't see it that way at all.'

'Communicating with the other departments is the difficulty; they seem to have a different set of values.'

and the sad:

'When I was a worker I knew the score. Now I seem to be judged on the basis of not being noticed. It's hard.'

The next two chapters are concerned with the organisation and the problems it inflicts on the New Manager. The people we meet often find themselves trapped between organisational re-organisations: somebody in top management decides to change organisational style and the New Managers have to face the music. Chapter 9 takes on organisational theory and tackles problems such as:

'When I joined the organisation I knew where I was.'

'Information flow is always down – never up.'

'They *tell* me, but when it comes to getting work out of my staff *telling* isn't the answer.'

'The staff have each other to talk to – I haven't.'

'I seem to be in a sort of bottleneck: upstairs they talk to one another, below they negotiate. Me? Well you tell me.'

Chapter 10 continues to stem the flow of problem issues about the manager in the organisation, and discusses the hybrid systems so popular in today's changing world.

'I've been told the theories of Taylor, Mayo, Maslow, Marx, and even the Japanese. Life is simply not like that.'

'I've been told that I have to be a consultative manager – *told*, mind you.'

'We seem to spend all our time consulting.'

'I work in what they call a matrix – fine for the first year, but now I seem to have lost all contact with the people for whom I have line responsibility.'

'We try everything – somebody goes on a course and we try it.'

'We used to have a sort of club atmosphere here, it was nice. Now it's all change all the time.'

'The retirement age will be before we join soon.'

Sometimes I worry about the depth of feeling behind the problem statements that I get. Chapter 11 considers the manager as change agent:

'It happens so fast: you're just getting in touch with the last reorganisation when the next one comes.'

'Problems come from two sides – individuals crack up and the whole team reacts pretty oddly.'

'Not everyone reacts the same way. You tell them they are redundant and some say "Yippee", others collapse.'

'How do you manage change when you are as much involved as the rest?'

The last chapter will attempt the impossible and bring together all the strands. I believe that:

'When all is said and done, there is more said than done.'

and therefore I am asking you to make definite and specific plans to experiment with, and to use, what you have read in this book.

The book is based on problem issues I have been given by New Managers. It is a world of many problems, and perhaps we had better get on with the journey of discussing many, and hopefully solving some, as soon as possible. Let's start the journey.

CHAPTER TWO

Knowing Yourself

'I never seem to be able to judge the effect my words have on other people.'

'If I can see people it's OK, but when I have to use the telephone or – worse still – write, then the trouble starts.'

'There is never any time to plan; things just happen and I have to react.'

'I know that I intend to be seen as a model of probity, but others seem to see me as some kind of monster.'

'Somebody always takes my written memos the wrong way.'

In the first chapter I referred to the concept of the management helicopter. I said that a major skill of any manager was to be able to act appropriately whatever the circumstances. I said that total involvement with the people with whom we work, while possible before the transition to manager, was virtually impossible for the effective manager. The manager is directing resources, including people, towards a goal. At times, for effective direction, this means that the manager needs to rise above the immediate situation, as if in a helicopter, and to view the whole scene. The individual needs and groups needs of his or her staff have to be seen in the total perspective of medium — and long-term goals. The management graffiti that comes to mind is: 'When you are up to your neck in alligators, it's difficult to remember that you came in to drain the swamp.'

I said that a major difficulty preventing the helicopter from being able to rise out of the mud was an inappropriate level of understanding between you and your subordinates. The New Manager is likely to have to make decisions where there is a conflict of interest between individuals and the most effective attainment of the goal; and, much more stressfully, to have to implement decisions from an authority with which he or she has limited sympathy. If the manager's limited sympathy with what he or she is attempting to implement is common knowledge, then the implementation will be that much harder. For you, each level in the hierarchy requires a delicate balance between what you wish to divulge about yourself to those around you and what you don't. A major readjustment has to be considered in the transition from managed to manager.

In the first chapter I discussed the concept of a window between you and the organisational world. The window has a clear section allowing all to see in, a shuttered section, and a blackened section. The control of what you hope to keep behind each section depends very much on how much you know about yourself. Others may know your strengths and weaknesses better than you do. Control of the window also relies vitally on your ability to communicate: if you cannot communicate cleanly to others, no amount of self-knowledge will be of any avail:

'Honestly, that wasn't what I meant to say at all'

is a statement that should be made as little as possible. This second chapter will begin to discuss the issue of communication.

Getting yourself across – communication

I suspect that all of us have had to write a difficult personal letter and finished with a full wastepaper basket. If we dare to look through the failures, some will have obvious mechanical faults – words misspelt, grammar less than perfect, coffee stains – but there will be more subtle classes of failure. Some of the crumpled sheets will have been rejected because 'it doesn't quite say what we mean to get over', and we may have to search hard in our hearts to clarify exactly what it was we meant to get over. Other crumpled sheets are 'open to misinterpretation if we get them in the wrong mood'. The perfect 'difficult' letter has to contain more than the simple message: it has to say how we felt when we wrote it *and* tell the recipient how we hope he or she will take the message.

'Darling, I want you to be brave. Unfortunately I have to tell you . . .'

Face to face we would not have had the same problem. As we came into the room our stance, our walk, our eyes would have told an aware person that we had a sad message to convey and that we had compassion for the person in the room. The line is from a hundred black and white B movies:

'It's all right, you don't need to say anything. It's John isn't it?'

'Yes, it is John,' and innumerable actresses in négligés touch us gently on the sleeve and ask for a few minutes' quiet before they allow the director to get on with the plot. In real life, the aware person intending to give a 'difficult' message to somebody attempts to judge the moment and fine-tune the words to the mood of the recipient. He or she may well also employ a considerable amount of 'stage management'.

————————▶

EXERCISE

Imagine you are a doctor who is expecting a second visit from a Peter West, a patient in his early thirties. Peter is recently married and the couple's first baby is on the way. He has everything to live for, but unfortunately the test you ran after his first visit indicated a very serious problem indeed. At best, your patient will need to undergo a series of tests as an in-patient in the local hospital. You are aware of the clinic within which you work and the effect it has on patients. Through the stiff double-doors they are greeted by the starched receptionist at a VDU, who judges her performance on efficiency and not compassion. Once registered, the patients wait, seated back to back around a central column, until a light shows on one of several doors. The door greeting your patients leads to a short but dim corridor, and you sense that several of them have even tried to visit a broom cupboard before getting to you. Normally, your clients are in a state of mild shock by the time you meet them.

How do you tell Peter?

What is your objective in the consultation?
What must you achieve and what would it be nice to achieve?

What is Peter's likely response?

How do you propose to achieve your object?
What is your personal approach?
Can you engineer improved rapport in some way?

What do you intend to communicate?
What is the doctor's objective in the consultation?

——————————▶

Again in terms of management graffiti:

> If you don't know where you are going
> you will finish up somewhere else.

Rule Number One in communication:

KNOW WHAT YOU INTEND TO COMMUNICATE.

The doctor may have decided that he must get Peter to understand that the symptoms are real and that the test already conducted needs to be confirmed. The best place for this confirmation is the local hospital. The doctor does not want Peter to get unduly frightened, but he does want him to be prepared and to think. He would like Peter to talk to his wife, and if possible to arrange for support during her confinement should Peter be out of action. If he has trouble getting Peter to accept reality, then the doctor is aware that the Social Services will arrange for support.

How does the doctor expect Peter to take the message? Well, at best Peter could find that his fears were grounded and that his seeking professional help was justified. At worst, Peter could jump to the conclusion that he was being treated as a child and that he was really going to die nastily. The key to how the doctor needs to behave is in that phrase, 'being treated as a child'. Is Peter likely to think he is being treated as a child? Looking at the clinic from the eyes of a patient, the answer is *Yes*. The parent figure of the receptionist, the frightening wait, the buzzer system and the dim corridor – these are all images that any person not feeling really assertive and confident is bound to see as a put-down. Even the most assertive and confident adult is likely to feel bad in such circumstances, and Peter is unlikely to be either. He has already been worried enough to seek advice in the first place, and now following the test he has had a period in which to imagine all forms of blackness. He is likely to be reliving all the fears of his actual childhood, and in that state the doctor is unlikely to get the sensible message across. Little people *feel*, and don't *listen* all that well.

The problem for the doctor is to reduce the frightened feeling from childhood that is likely to be taking over the persona of the adult he wishes to meet. OK, he will try to meet Peter in a

comparatively quiet time and arrange to greet him personally so as
to cut out the waiting-room trauma. He will inform the receptionist that he wants to be told immediately when Peter checks in,
and that he will meet him at the desk. He will take Peter into the
surgery and not sit behind any desk. He will look Peter in the eyes
and tell him the facts as they are . . .
Fine, if you have the time. Rule Number two:

MAKE THE TIME TO PLAN

It is the easiest excuse in the world to say that you have no time to
communicate effectively:

'There was no time to do all that planning; it just happened.'

Fine sometimes; but comparatively rarely is it impossible to take a
breath and think:

What am I trying to achieve and, having achieved that, what
would I like to achieve next?

What is the likely response of the other person?

How ought I to structure my behaviour to best achieve my
objective?

What we need to do is to be able to read both ourselves and other
people pretty quickly. In 'real life', without additional skills we do
misread ourselves and others. We find that, when we expect to be
facing a rational adult, we meet a screaming child. We find that we
see ourselves as acting as models of probity, while others see us as
prejudiced and critical parental figures. Our communication, if
recorded verbatim by a secretary, would be sensible; but when we
look at the whole picture – our stance and our position combined
with our tone of voice and our words – we could be coming over
inappropriately to others. Communication is complex and the
human computer views the whole picture, not just the spoken
words. Imagine an actor being given a line from an unknown play.
The words on the page could be as simple as, 'I need you.' These
could be said softly as a caress by a lover, or brutishly by a bully.
The personality of the character, his or her relation to the
recipient, the mood of the play, the stance of the personalities, all
would contribute to the communication.

The channels of human communication

When we attempt to write a difficult letter we feel awkward and

restricted because we are only able to use part of our communications system. When we communicate face to face we are able to
convey a great deal more that just the words we speak. Whether
we intend it or not, the tone of our voice, our facial expression, our
hands, the direction of our gaze, our body posture and positioning
all contribute to communication. The actual words spoken,
depending on the situation, play only a very small part in the total
communication.

─────────▶

EXERCISE

Using television programmes, attempt to log the 'media' being
used. Take two contrasting situations – perhaps a politician
being interviewed on a 'difficult' subject, and a scene in a
romantic play where two actors are suggesting approaching
intimacy.

Log the 'media' signals you pick up:

The starting orientation – face to face, side by side . . .?

Changes in orientation – what caused the change, and what
happened?

Eye contact – is there avoidance, is it short or is it long?

Body postures – relaxed, tense, do the body postures match
each other?

Changes in posture – what caused the change?
Use of hands – clenched, protective, violent, wagging fingers
. . .

Facial expressions – smiles and frowns, were they in tune with
the rest of the communications?

Tones of voice – do you believe the words now?

Try the same exercise in a public place.

When you are communicating on a one-to-one basis, where are
you concentrating your effort – words, tone, stance . . .?

─────────▶

On looking back at the television exercise, it is interesting to
remember that films worked quite well before the invention of

sound. A good actor – and we may say manager, or even, simply, human being – presents a complete set of messages that other people interpret. If you find yourself being misinterpreted, it is well worth working in front of a mirror, or better still, in front of a video camera. You may find that your hair or your glasses obscure your eyes. Or you may find that your dress is over-severe or over-frivolous, and does not reflect the way you feel. Look with the eyes and ears of the other person.

Now one of the issues with which I headed this chapter was concerned with telephone and written communication. The telephone is a partial communicator, and the written word is something completely different. Let's discuss the telephone first.

> When I ran a training centre my secretary was responsible for, among other things, telephone sales. She was superb. Sometimes I would watch her at work, dialling from a list of potential clients. As a human being she was lovely, but on the phone she was a professional. Every intonation of her voice implied wrapt attention, almost – in the case of male clients – a suggestion of seduction. Her actions while she purred down the phone were totally different – she would be doing her nails, eating a sandwich or even reading a knitting pattern. She had a total understanding of the channels of communication. If only two – words and tone – are being followed, get them right and don't waste effort on the unobserved.

(I am aware that some schools teaching telephone sales demand of their pupils full 'face-to-face' gestures while speaking down the mouthpiece, and certainly this is likely to be better for a beginner; but I have found that many skilled operators take a pride in not following the advice.) The telephone conversation gives the communicator very little chance to observe feedback. When we say something heavy, we cannot notice the recoil; when we say something warming, we cannot see whether the other person moves slightly towards us. We cannot encourage the other person by mirroring his or her gestures, and we cannot 'conduct' the other person with our hands.

If you watch a skilled communicator you will see that he or she uses a plethora of non-verbal techniques to emphasise, to encourage and to control. The telephone reduces these techniques to what can be called NCGs – non-committal grunts and silences. The skilled communicator knows whether he or she wishes to communicate with the 'little person' and be treated in awe, or with the 'reasoning adult' and get real discussion, or simply to exchange prejudice with another critical parent figure.

The medium of the written word is technically more restricted than the telephone and can only guarantee one channel – the words themselves. It cannot guarantee how and when the words are being read, or the audience that is reading them. It probably cannot even guarantee that the words are seen in the complete context or in the format intended. For example, there is the story of a newspaper critic who hated a particular London play and wrote: 'A technically perfect play and a good night's entertainment, provided you hate acting and originality.' Outside the theatre on the play bills his words had been reduced to: 'A technically perfect play and a good night's entertainment . . .'

We do not need a deliberate attempt at deception by our audience to bring about the wrong meaning. We are very capable of sabotaging ourselves. As I have said before, the skilled verbal, face-to-face communicator knows what mood, what state of mind he or she wants, or indeed expects, in the recipient. I use the phrases 'little person', 'rational adult' and 'parental figure' to describe moods or states of mind. When the skilled communicator finds not what he or she expects but perhaps prejudice instead of rationality, then he or she makes rapid adjustments to the communication style. You can never say, 'Sorry, this is obviously the wrong moment' when things have gone wrong. What you have written is already on the notice-board or has been sent to the union head office. Rule Number Three for all communication, but overwhelmingly for written communication:

KEEP IT SIMPLE.

The English language is immensely rich in words able to express nuances of meaning beyond the basic connotation. The problem for the writer of business communications is that nuances are unsuited for the buckshot approach of standard communication. One person's subtle nuance may well mean different things to different people, and sometimes the technically unspoken meaning becomes transparent.

Suppose, for example, we feel that there is an element of ignorance in the behaviour of our workforce and decide to write a memorandum to convey our feelings. We may decide, quite rightly, that the word 'ignoramus' is a bit strong and look for synonyms in *Roget:*

Ignoramus – know-nothing, illiterate, no scholar, low brow, duffer, dunce, greenhorn, novice, new, beginner, simpleton, bebe, innocent, dupe . . .

Our choice of word, however we may dispute the exactness of the synonyms given by Roget, tells us a great deal about our intended relationship with other people. It is as if, by using certain words, we conjure up images in people's minds, and this image formation blocks logical acceptance of what we intend to get over. If we intended to communicate down to 'little people' – to tell them that we are in charge and they had better do what we say – we could call them 'greenhorns' in our memorandum and the imagery conjured up by the word would convey exactly our feelings about our staff. But conveying the exact relationship we had in mind is dangerous even if we can witness the response, but likely to be fatal in the more permanent medium of the written word. However we feel about our staff, a much safer choice of words would be 'new to the job'. Choose 'unloaded' words as far as possible and try to appeal to the rational adult in the audience. Whether the recipient is 'new' to a particular endeavour or not is probably a question of undisputed fact. Whether or not he is a 'dunce' or a 'greenhorn' is likely to arouse controversy well outside the meaning you wish to convey. The following is pretty straightforward:

> Recent accidents with forklift trucks have led us to review our authorising procedures. In future all new operators will need to complete a training course and obtain a proficiency certificate authorised by Personnel. All existing operators should see their departmental managers as soon as possible.

Try:

> Recent accidents have been caused by greenhorns driving forklift trucks. In future everyone will have to prove they can drive the things and produce a certificate authorised by Personnel saying just that. Get trained, you greenhorns, we don't want any more accidents. It's costing the MD too much in repair bills for his car already.

Fun perhaps, but not taken as such by the staff of the factory concerned. Possibly the bluff machismo-style manager could get away with this sort of joky presentation with eye-to-eye contact; in writing, it is poison. Imagine this form of 'fun' instruction faded on a company notice-board weeks after the event. We can agree that the joke approach is probably over the top for most circumstances, but there is something else – the word 'greenhorn'. How does he see his staff if he uses the word 'greenhorn'? When we hear the word we get flashing through our heads a series of images of western bars, gun-shooters and cheroots chewed at the base.

Male, tough and phoney; and therefore we reject the message and begin to look for ways of rejecting it logically.

The four rules of communication I will repeat are:

> KNOW WHAT YOU INTEND TO COMMUNICATE
> MAKE TIME TO PLAN
> KEEP IT SIMPLE
> KEEP IT SHORT

and I will add another:

> KNOW YOUR AUDIENCE – DON'T WRITE GLOBALLY

A recent advertisement for Epsom computer systems put it very simply:

> Your main aim in writing business letters should be to keep them as short as possible. This will not only save you time, but will also improve the chances of your letter being read and acted upon.
> Follow the example of the French general who sent this message to a courtesan in Paris: 'Ou? Quand? Combien?' He soon received the reply: 'Chez moi. Ce soir. Rien.' – and duly did the business.

————▶

EXERCISE

Look at the three statements below as being part of a written memo and attempt to visualise your reception after using each form of words.

I have to leave the plant	unattended empty without staff unmanned inadequately staffed
Your work is	not adequate not good enough not as agreed giving us problems
The factory is not	making money making sufficient money profitable viable

Put yourself in the other's shoes.

What would you as the receiver see as the objective of each message, and how would you see the way the sender sees you?

What images does each form of work conjure up?

Let's take one of the examples – 'The factory is not . . .' I would see the statement 'The factory is not making money' as a pure statement of fact. What comes after such a line is likely to be a reasoned case of why this is so, without any judgements. The reader is respected by the writer.

The sentences increase in unarguable judgement, and any employee reading 'The factory is not viable' would be wise to reach across for the 'Situations Vacant' columns. Your reaction would also depend very much on your status in the company when you read some of the statements. Imagine reading 'The factory is not sufficiently profitable' as a manager. The manager could well see a detailed case emerging, with various proposals for reduced expenditure and increased efficiency generally. It's going to be a hard time but at least we will be busy. Take yourself back to the shop floor and ask what the phrase means to you. It could well mean threats of cut-backs – overtime, petty cheese-paring and redundancies. From the shop floor we could well predict trouble, and we may see ourselves losing our jobs. Understanding how to interpret what you read or hear all depends on where you are in the hierarchy. 'Viable' will worry the managers, and 'sufficiently profitable', the staff. You have to know your audience, and writing globally leads to problems.

When you have total empathy with your audience, then communication can move into code. People in empathy can listen to the way we begin a sentence and predict the way the sentence is going to . . . end. The structure both of written and of spoken language and the previous knowledge the people involved have of each other contribute significantly to the information content, to such a point that information richness can become information redundancy in many messages. Think of those office or shop-floor conversations over coffee where everyone seems to be able to cut each other's conversations so that, for the outsider, no sentence ever seems to be completed:

'The trouble with workers today is . . .'
'I know, I was only saying to the MD yesterday about the new graduates . . .'

'Were you on university graduate milk round this year?'

The practice of over-cutting and the use of jargon provide a formidable barrier to the New Manager who has not yet attained the 'in group' in an organisation. It is something that has to be borne until somehow you find you can join in, first perhaps by discovering that the 'milk round' is a journey round chosen universities and colleges to interview new graduates, and *then* to choose *your* time for joining the conversation. Imagine yourself like the child listening to his elders and betters at the dinner table; bide your time and come in gently:

'It was my first time on the milk round for recruitment this year. Are you saying that what we found wasn't typical?'

If they answer you, then you are in.

In the next chapter we will extend our understanding by developing a language to see more into the words and the gestures that bring out the music behind the words.

CHAPTER THREE

Communication

Us and *Them* of communication – where it goes wrong and what to do about it

'Psychology might be able to help me if it wasn't for that terrible jargon.'

'I find myself getting into pointless rows.'

'I try to be consistent when I give instructions. Sometimes they do what I say, sometimes they just get angry, and sometimes I can see that they're just waiting for me to be out of the way.'

'My boss tries to be always nice, and everyone gets hurt.'

'My problem is giving instructions to different people; I just do not judge the best way.'

'I can hear people say "Well, if that's how you feel you'd better do it yourself."'

'If I can see people it's OK, but when I have to use the telephone or – worse still – write, then the trouble starts.'

That last 'issue' is a carry-over from Chapter 2: we are still on the problems of human communications, but this time we are going to explore a way of codifying those magic words – 'States of Mind'. I have explained that the states of mind of people attempting communication are fundamental to understanding the processes of effective communication. If the person initiating implies a particular state of mind, and my example was the use of the word 'greenhorn', then the tone of the communication is set. A critical state of mind in the initiator will trigger responses from the receiver ranging from total subservience to aggression. I discussed how a doctor might demonstrate that, in spite of expectations, he wished to communicate to a patient in an adult way. In the second chapter I struggled with the language I used, and was very conscious of the issue that began this chapter:

'Psychology might be able to help me if it wasn't for that terrible jargon.'

I agree, and will begin this chapter by correcting the fault.

An end to the terrible jargon

In the closing days of the Second World War, Dr Eric Berne was responsible for signing the discharge papers of a large number of American sailors. Apart from deciding whether they had any socially transferable disease, he also had to decide whether they were sound in mind. Watching thousands of sailors for a few minutes, and putting his name to thousands of documents with a reasonable degree of certainty, got him to ask the question – How? How was it possible to look at people for a few seconds and judge their sanity? He kept the question in his mind when he went into private practice as a psychoanalyst, recognising that the one major block between himself and his clients was language. The words of Freud were not the words of everyday experience.

Eric Berne recognised that there are three overall classifications for the *states of mind* of human beings. The clinical psychology of his day used language outside and away from an everyday context, and so Berne called his 'States of Mind' Parent, Adult and Child. Berne's use of these words to classify the states of mind of his patients is parallel, not identical, to the way we use them in everyday life. Even so, the words can be used to discuss human communication between ordinary healthy people.

--------------►

EXERCISE

Put down the words Parent, Adult and Child as headings on sheets of paper, and list the concepts you associate with them, thus:

Parent
Orders
Authority
Concern
. . . .

Do not get trapped into thinking of the functions of real live parents – father, mother – but think of the behaviours you associate with the roles.

When you have completed your list, compare your notes with mine.

———————————▶

The lists I have collected from managers look something like this:

Parent	Adult	Child
Orders	Rational	Fun
Authority	Logical	Love and sex
Teacher	Calculating	Taught
Warm, loving	Computing	Rebellious
Standards	Dull, boring	Cute
Caring	Problem-solving	Malleable
Prejudiced	Unemotional	Emotional
Critical	Here and now	Manipulative
Nursing		Untouched
Responsible		Irresponsible
Concern		Sly
		Accepting

The words I have eliminated from my lists are those that lead us to think of the Parent as a person with children, of the Adult as having certain age limits, and of the Child as someone who grows up – not only children are childish. In the Berne model, the words Parent, Adult and Child have very specific meanings, states of mind with the attributes given in the lists and which are shown by all of us to varying degrees when called upon. In developing his language of human communication, Berne saw that Parent concepts fell into two patterns – those associated with criticism, the wagging finger, and those associated with nurturing – and he gave them suitable titles the main category of Parent. He called them the *Critical Parent* and the *Nurturing* or *Caring Parent*.

Parent

Critical	Nurturing
Authority	Caring
Orders	Concern
Standards	Warm, loving
Prejudice	Nursing

The Child concepts also seemed to fit into sub-categories, three this time:

Child

Natural	Adapted	Manipulative (Little Professor)
Fun	Taught	Cute
Love and sex	Malleable	Creative
Emotional	Rebellious	Sly
Irresponsible	Accepting	Manipulative
Untouched		
Innocent		

The Adult concepts were left undivided. Berne put the total model into diagrammatic form:

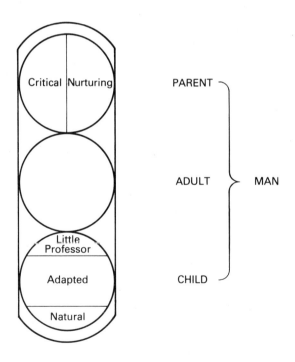

The first point that needs to be emphasised is that *all* of us can act from any of these states of mind, given the right personal circumstances. The second point is that most of us prefer particular states and are inclinded to act from them more frequently.

Suppose we have been working on a particular project and have just been told that it has failed. We could reply expressing each of the three states, and indeed, each of the sub-divisions. Let's try:

'Your project has failed' – 'I told you and you wouldn't listen.' *Our fingers are wagging and we are frowning; we are in Critical Parent mode.*

'Your project has failed.' – 'Don't worry, it will be OK'. *We feel almost compelled to touch the bearer of bad news, to comfort him for having a difficult job. We are in Nurturing Parent.*

'Your project has failed.' – 'We need to find out how many other people are concerned and let them know. Then perhaps . . .' *Our stance is straight and we are looking the messenger straight in the eye. We are in Adult.*

'Your project has failed. – 'Oh dear, still I never signed anything so with luck someone else will carry the can.' *We have a sly little grin and maybe wink because we are in Child – Little Professor.*

'Your project has failed.' – 'Not again!' or 'That does it!' *In either case we may well be looking down, with our toes slightly turned in. Both are a give-away for Adapted Child – compliant first and rebellious second.*

'Your project has failed.' – '! ! ! ! !' (Expletive deleted). *We stamp our foot and tell the world that we are in Natural Child. We could also have suddenly seen the funny side of things, or even started to cry – all in Natural Child.*

I myself could give all of these responses, expressing any of the states of mind and initiated by the neutrally spoken phrase, 'Your project has failed'. Since my response in some cases is far from neutral, I may in return initiate very varied reactions in the others present.

You would have a very good clue as to my state of mind from listening to my words, but much more importantly, by *watching* me. The Critical Parent stands differently and the eyes are hard; the Nurturing Parent seems to reach out to care for you; the Adult catches your eye; and the Child looks defensive, cheeky, defiant or shifty. All of us have been people-watching for years and, to survive, have had to become pretty good at it. We are so good at it that we are rather like the skilled typist who cannot vocalise the position of letters on a keyboard but *knows* them without thinking. However, to improve on our human communications, I believe the 'vocalising' process of putting names to things actually helps. To Berne the new titles were a revelation. He was able to understand how it was possible for him to look briefly at his demobbed sailors and make his mind up about them: he had a common language to codify behaviour and to develop a popularising of psychology that enabled ordinary people to attain new insights and new skills. It is the language of Berne's *Parent, Adult* and *Child* that I shall use throughout this book to clarify and discuss events and issues.

――――――▶

EXERCISE

Analysing States of Mind

Think back to the Man/Woman-watching exercises in the previous chapter.

What clues – words, gestures, postures and attitudes – do you have to indicate the states of mind of the people you watched? You may of course 'cheat' and think of other occasions when you were able to look down from your 'helicopter' and observe the people around you.

Parent. Give specific words and actions that indicated the people you were observing were in the Parent state of mind.

....
....
....

Adult. Give specific words and actions that indicated the people you were observing were in the Adult state of mind.

....
....
....

Child. Give specific words and actions that indicated the people you were observing were in the Child state of mind.

....
....
....

If someone was observing you, and they certainly will have been, what state of mind would they have found predominant?

....

What would have been the clues they picked up to decide on this?

How would their observations affect the way they react to you?

――――――▶

All these states of mind are with all of us, but perhaps we do not find them all appropriate at work. Perhaps we would worry if the Natural Child appeared too often or even if the Natural Child was known to exist at all in work (though your colleagues probably knew it well when you were on the shop floor, at the blackboard or on the bench). The people you worked with before your translation to management probably knew a great deal about all your states of mind, and here you are as a manager trying to give instructions from Critical Parent. They may know that you are very strong in Nurturing Parent – a nice person to work with, but a big softy as a manager. Alternatively, they could have known you as preferring to act from the Adult state of mind, and realise that they can always get you as a manager to see both sides of the question when a clear firm decision in Critical Parent would be more appropriate. The manager needs to be able to act appropriately, from the state of mind most suited to the total circumstances of the situation. Anyone who sticks too strongly to a preferred state of mind had problems as a communicator.

A very interesting exercise in a workshop course for New Managers involves asking six people to act out a short scene where each person *stays* in a particular state of mind throughout. The plot involves a manager who needs to make sure the plant/school/ office is manned during the summer months. All his or her subordinates have unfortunately already booked their holidays for the same weeks and the manager has to sort the situation out whilst staying in Nurturing Parent, and so the personality requires him or her to:

Nurture.

Rescue people when any form of conflict is likely to start.

Offer help, whether it is required or not.

Support the people and not the ideas they may be putting forward.

The manager who is locked in Nurturing Parent is a disaster as a manager because he or she is totally unable to take the long view, to disentangle the helicopter and fly above the immediate people issues. Always something comes up to prevent the wider – the long-term – view, and the short-term rescue takes over. The Nurturing Parent manager will assume the role of an archetypal social worker, and there is no limit to the problems a workforce

Some indicators of the states of mind people are in would be:

Words	Voice	Gestures	Attitude
Critical parent			
Must	Condescending	Pointing finger	Judgemental
Always	Superior	Folded arms	Opinionated
Never	Critical	Hard eyes	Adamant
Nurturing parent			
Well done	Caring	Open arms	Responding
That's nice	Loving	Pat on head	Protective
Take care	Worried	Arm on shoulder	Nurturing
Adult			
Why/what/where?	Questioning	Straight posture	Analytical
How/when?	Thoughtful	Measured	Unemotional
Can we find out?	Even	Direct	Detached
Child – Little Professor			
Maybe	Childlike	Finger on nose	Detached
If only	Hesitant	Head on side	Manipulative
But you said	Innocent	Eyes irregular	Selfish
Child – Adapted/acceptant			
Sorry	Downcast	Self-protective	Compliant/clown
Please	Whingeing	Eyes downcast	Acceptant
Could I?	Hopeful	Waiting	Eager to please
Child – Adapted/rebellious			
No!	Defiant	Stamping foot	Rebellion
Won't!	Sharp	Quick frown	Negativity
Go away!	Measured	Head turn	Final
Child – Natural or Free			
Super!	Expressive	Wide	Unconcerned
I'd love to	Direct	Uninhibited	ME!
Wow!	Private	Dancing	For today

can find if pressed. Deadlines will not be met and the staff will never develop, with the independent souls leaving for more challenging climes.

The others in the exercise are also asked to stay in a particular state of mind, and the one thing that happens is that the problems remain unresolved. The basic lesson is that anyone – manager or subordinate – who stays in a particular state of mind regardless of what else is happening, is impossible to work with. The Parent-locked managers or subordinates are concerned only with prejudice and how things were in the past; the Child-locked managers never initiate anything and are totally egocentric; the Adult who, without all this noise of people, might get a logical solution never gets heard and almost invariably gets angry and moves into Critical Parent.

In 'real life' people locked in particular states of mind are rare, certainly in a world outside therapy; but most of us have a preferred state of mind and have been known to work from this state through thick and thin, ignoring the problems such behaviour causes.

The Critical Parent-dominated manager will get things done, but is inclined to see things in black and white. There is a great tendency to blame and to instruct without hearing the issues out. There will almost be a glorying in conflicts and a great tendency towards judgement. Here is the manager who is happy to describe staff as 'greenhorns'. As with the Nurturing Parent manager, the staff will not develop and the manager may well find that he or she ends up doing all the work around while the staff say:

'Well, if that's how you feel you'd better do it yourself.'

The manager locked inappropriately in Adult will miss all the human issues, concentrating on the *task* and ignoring the *process*. Getting on with the task is so obvious for the Adult-dominated manager that he or she will be amazed that other people have other priorities. I know of one such Adult-dominated manager whose subordinate suffered a major bereavement in the middle of a rather heavy work schedule. The subordinate asked a friend to cover for a few hours while he consoled his mother. When he returned to the office he heard his boss's public comments:

'Why do people have to have relations? I wish people would see there is a job to be done.'

Relations, in the other sense, were never the same again in the department. To those who do not share a strong Adult mode, the Adult-dominated manager appears at best cold and boring. The Adult-dominated manager very often moves into Critical Parent when the going gets tough.

All the Child-dominated states of mind present difficult problems for subordinates. The Adapted Child manager does not reflect local problems in the department back to superiors, but simply agrees. He or she is also open to lobbying – the last person to blow in his or her ear gets their way.

Dr Blue was the head of a company development department which was known not to be performing to company requirements. In discussion with his staff many issues came out, but the one that sticks in my mind was concerned with the allocation of space. When a project was requested by Head Office it came through Dr Blue and was accepted without question. He would then call upon relevant staff and say:

'I know you are all busy but it has to be done. Head Office wants you to drop everything and get on with it.'

'OK if you say so – I want Process Building Number 2.'

'Of course.'

The next day another member of staff would find that he had lost Process Building Number 2 and would go to see Blue.

'Look I need Process Building Number 2 for . . .'

'Of course you do . . . sort it out with the others.'

An Adapted Child-dominated manager such as Dr Blue is never proactive: his is a style of working that might be effective in a supervisor or specialist but is weak in a manager. The Natural Child manager is very difficult, but at times fun to work with; the Little Professor has to be watched; but both of them are inclined to be brilliantly creative at times.

---------►

EXERCISE

Think about the jobs below, and the energy likely in each of the states of mind. Mark High, Medium and Low – thus:

	CP	NP	A	LP	AC	NC
TV Games Host	H	—	—	H	L	H+

I see a lot of energy in the Critical Parent state of mind, which is inclined to get nasty if challenged. The job is manipulative and basically 'over the top', hence the Little Professor and Natural Child. The TV host always looks as if criticism would be taken badly, so I have scored the energy in Adapted Child as low.

Now try:

	CP	NP	A	LP	AC	NC
Traffic Warden						
Data Processing Manager						
Social Worker						
Technical Teacher						
Programmer						

CP – Critical Parent NP – Nurturing Parent A – Adult
LP – Little Professor AC – Adapted Child NC – Natural Child

What sort of ideas led you to your decisions about the likely profiles?

What would be your own ideal profile before promotion, and what would be your own ideal as a New Manager?

Is there a major difference between the ideals before and after promotion?

What would you see as the likely effects of such a change on you as a person?

————————▶

With regard to the first part of the exercise let's take a frivolous look at a Traffic Warden, with apologies to any real wardens who happen to be reading the book.

	CP	NP	A	LP	AC	NC
Traffic Warden	H	–	–	H	H	–

My logic is as follows. There are few more Critical Parent activities than standing writing down details of cars with a pencil. Any appeal to reason, or certainly mercy, is likely to be ignored – the job goes by the book, so it's high Adapted Child and zero Nurturing Parent and Adult. We know the Adapted Child is high anyway, because we saw the Mayor's car being ignored when it was parked next to ours and we got a fine. The Little Professor is demonstrated by the way wardens seem to hide behind a pillar when we are parking and suddenly leap out when we go. There is no joy in them, so we do not rate Natural Child.

I have found that the stereotypes I have of other people's jobs seldom meet reality, but perhaps I may have had some luck with my own job, before and after the great transition. The point I have found a hundred times was put like this in the first chapter: 'I then found that to progress I had to become a manager. I had to search for new skills, to flex muscles in my personality that had had no previous work experience.'

The specialist, the worker, the managed can afford to concentrate his or her energies in the job on restricted elements of personality while doing the job. The production supervisor can rely strongly on Critical Parent, the programmer on Adult, the ward orderly on Nurturing Parent, and the actor on Natural Child. The actor-manager needs all the personality to survive – the Critical Parent to discipline others and meet deadlines, the Nurturing Parent to protect confused staff, the Adult to sort out the finances. The Natural Child actor may have the other aspects of personality as a parent or as perhaps a sportsman, but as an actor-manager *all the states of mind will be required at some time for the job*. His or her home or leisure life may well suffer.

I know of many male managers who, before promotion as specialists, found no need for Nurturing Parent at work and made excellent loving fathers at home. With promotion they found that the new job took all their available energy in Nurturing Parent, and that very little indeed was available for their home lives. They had to completely re-negotiate their relationships with their spouses. I know of one manager who was promoted to a senior personnel job during a time of major company crisis and found himself unable to deal with even minor issues where a gentle hand on the arm and a concerned use of time was essential. I will be going back to this point in the next chapter.

Freud and later Berne had the concept of a total person having their energies wrapped up in the various states of mind. The idea is that the total energy a person has in each state is his or her potential to react in that state. The potential energy can be seen as that locked up in a monkey collecting coconuts from a high tree. All the potential energy may be converted by one single dive to the ground for one coconut; or more sensibly, by the wise monkey, in a series of controlled leaps to many coconuts. The sudden release of all one's potential energy into Critical Parent can be compared to the diving monkey. Wise monkeys and wise managers do not act that way and, incidentally, collect more coconuts.

Remember the exercise we did in the second chapter about the doctor who wished to give potentially bad news to the patient.

Using the Berne Model, the dangerous 'transaction' was:
Critical Parent to Adapted Child. The doctor wanted to talk to a
rational being – the Adult in the Berne Model. Everything in the
environment led to the Adapted Child being the most likely person
to come through the surgery door.

Adapted Child *sees* others as Critical or Nurturing Parent
whether they wish to be in such a state of mind or not. The
Adapted Child is a part of personality that developed from the
little person of true childhood learning to cope with the world of
big people – the parent figures who are so successful. The doctor
decides on a strategy that allows him to 'meet the Adult'.

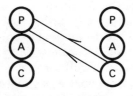   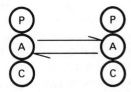

Likely Transaction   *Preferred Transaction*

In any transaction between individuals, there is inclined to be one
person who is allowed to choose the pattern of the communication. One person feels 'down' (Adapted Child), and the others may
easily slip into persecution (Critical Parent), or rescue (Nurturing
Parent). When we are in the Adapted Child part of our personality
we do not think about the here-and-now, but experience a *déjà vu*
in which we accept that someone else will take responsibility and
that we are not empowered to do anything by ourselves. The 'big'
people knew best in our childhood and still do now.

The Adapted Child will always adopt a reactive role – acceptant
to a point but, when pushed, rebellious. Very often in the
manager/subordinate relationship the manager is in either Critical
Parent or Nurturing Parent, and is in a position to determine the
course of the transaction.

'Do what you are told.'
'Yes sir.'
Critical Parent to an Adapted Child who
was available to answer the phone.

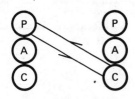

'Do what you are told.'
'Bog off!'
Adapted Child was able to answer the
phone, but the energy is in Rebellious
Child.

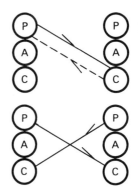

'Do what you are told.'
'Who are you to tell me . . .'
This time the manager has missed
any Adapted Child and meets
another Critical Parent.
We have trouble.

The same issues happen when we work from Nurturing Parent.
'Let me do it for you' could result in exactly the same set of
responses. The responses to Critical Parent and Nurturing Parent
Managers are archaic – memories of people and environments
from the past and of the most effective way we responded to them
as little people. Critical Parent and Nurturing Parent are part of
the personality of good managers, but only part: the whole of the
personality needs to be represented for effective management.

————▶

EXERCISE

Think of your own work and the situations where each of the
states of mind – Nurturing and Critical Parent, Adult and the
Child states (Little Professor, Adapted and Natural Child) –
would be the preferred way of conducting the communication.

What from your own point of view would be the difficulties in
engineering the tranactions as you want them?

How could you best arrange things the way you want them?

Consider communications in the past where things have gone
wrong. Explain the problems in terms of the Berne model.

————————————▶

Giving instructions – the message and the people

I almost blush to have to say that the manager needs to be able to *tell* other people to do things. 'Get those sacks moved' works better than:

> 'We seem to be having a problem with the forklift trucks getting round the corner. Perhaps if you are not too busy you might be able to spend time moving those sacks into a place where . . .'

In the first example the manager is clear, brief and does not apologise for taking command. Other things being equal, he or she would be obeyed. In the second case the manager acts in a confused way, almost challenging others to demur, and is unlikely to be obeyed.

The first rules for giving instructions are:

TAKE RESPONSIBILITY

EXPECT TO BE OBEYED

KNOW WHAT YOU WANT

KEEP IT SIMPLE

If you are not clear and assertive, or do not take responsibility, or do not really know what you want, you come over in the Adapted Child state of mind and everything in your bearing will announce this. If you do not expect to be obeyed, it is unlikely that you will be. In our chapter on written communication we also discussed 'knowing your audience'; in verbal communication this is even more important. We can say a great deal more about this. It is possible to give instructions from all the states of mind and, we suspect, to all the states of mind of the managed; but the more useful transactions are:

> Critical Parent to Adult – *Directive:* 'These sacks are in the way – would you mind removing them straight away.'

> Nurturing Parent to Child – *Supportive:* 'You'd better move them for your own sake.'

> Adult to Adult – *Logical:* 'These sacks are in a dangerous place and it would be sensible if you moved them before the end of your stint.'

> Natural Child to Natural Child – *Emotive:* 'Come on, the place looks like a tip.'

The example I gave first was intended to be Critical Parent to Adult, but of course could be seen as Critical Parent to Adapted Child if we got our stance or tone wrong. If I had added a single word:

'Get those sacks moved – now.'

the Adapted Child would certainly know he or she had been addressed and would have been able to reply in Acceptant Adapted Child:

'Yes, certainly, OK.'

or Rebellious Adapted Child:

'Move them yourself.'

or as another Critical Parent:

'You can get somebody else to move them: you are not *my* manager and you ought to know that.'

————▶

EXERCISE

The styles of giving instructions are:

CP to A	Directive
NP to AC	Supportive
A to A	Logical
NC to NC	Emotive
(CP to AC	Interruptive)*

CP = Critical Parent A = Adult NP = Nurturing Parent
AC = Adapted Child NC = Natural Child

Imagine an incident where you have to tell a subordinate to come to work on time. Try to give instructions in each of the four styles.

In each style:

(a) How would you feel?

(b) How would the subordinate feel about you?

(c) What would be the short-term pay-off – would the effect be immediate?

---

*The interruptive style – CP to AC – is dangerous in practice and should only be used where the immediate pay-off outweighs all other considerations. An example might be an employee who is about to walk under a bus. In the analogy of the monkey gathering coconuts, Critical Parent to Adapted Child is inclined to get out of hand: all your potential energy can be converted to kinetic energy and you win one coconut at the expense of future crops.

(d) What would be the long-term pay-off for you and the
     organisation?

─────────────────────────▶

Alone in all the styles of giving instructions, the Critical Parent to
Adapted Child mode can trigger two disastrous alternative responses – Rebellious Child or a second Critical Parent. I suspect,
however, that it is the style most commonly used by the frustrated
inexperienced manager. All the other modes work – given the right
time, the right place and the right recipient. To understand the
right time, place and recipient, we need to know something about
the way in which we accept changes, and in particular changes
enforced by a manager who wants others to change their behaviour, do something different or do something new.

Any change is a disruption; and if we are to overcome this
disruption, we need to answer – in our heads at least – several
questions, the answers to which form a cycle. When all the
questions have been answered to our satisfaction, then the change
is made and we will modify our behaviour, drop what we are
doing and – in my example – 'move the sacks'. Suppose we are the
subordinate happily going about our business and we meet the
manager who wants us to move the sacks. First we need to know
why the sacks are to be moved. The reason could range from
'Why? Because I say so' to a very detailed explanation and some
very definite positive motivation in the form of a reward. We then
need to know something about *what* needs to be done. If we are
skilled, the direct instruction will lead us to take the sack back to
the appropriate department and collect a receipt to be filed in the
appropriate place. If we are new to the game, we will need to be
told all these things. And so it is with our next issue of *how*. The
skilled operator will not need to be told that the sacks are too
heavy to be moved by hand and that a forklift truck needs to be
collected using a works docket. But a new person will not know
this and will have problems with the order, however well motivated he or she may be. Finally, there may be some residual *'if'*
questions that need to be resolved – whether it is OK to leave our
present job to move the sacks, whether the sacks have been left by
someone else for a purpose, and even whether the manager has the
right to command their removal. All these questions need to be
considered, and they form a cycle (see opposite).

Obviously, in a matter as simple as the removal of some sacks we
would not expect to have to answer all these questions when

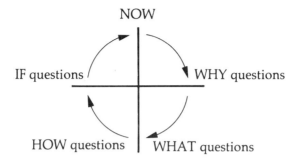

NOW

IF questions   WHY questions

HOW questions   WHAT questions

giving the command. Usually, some of the sectors of the cycle would have to be assumed, life being just too short for:

> 'These sacks are a danger to the safety of the plant and I am the Safety Officer. What I want you to do is take them round to the stores now and tell the storeman that I sent you. You will not attempt to lift them yourself, but find someone with a forklift and give them this note. While you are doing that I will clear it with your supervisor.'

However, silly as it may sound, a complete 'greenhorn' *would* need instructions in this form.

Why, *What*, *How* and *If* are the basic questions that concern anyone who has to tell anyone else to do something. The Natural Child coupled with Adult contains the curious part of our personality that needs the *Why* answers; the Adapted Child accepts the instructions for *What* is needed; and the Parent is concerned with the practicalities of *How* things should be done. If all of us were the same, giving instructions would be easy: *Why*, *What* and *How*, in that order, every time. We would motivate the Natural Child, satisfy the Adult, instruct the Adapted Child and lend authority to the Parent. But life is not like that. Two things make such a simple procedure impracticable: differences between jobs, and differences between people.

$\longrightarrow$

EXERCISE

> Consider these four very different individuals as subordinates needing your briefing.
>
> 1. Max is a computer systems architect who is able to see all the workings of a new machine and convert them into something that others can detail. It is a very creative job indeed. He is now working within a team

developing a new computer. He is a very talented individual who works in his own time, is sociable and belongs to several environmental groups. The rest of the team are now waiting for his contribution, but he simply does not seem to want to get down to it.

2. Mary is a senior chemical analyst who works with frightening intensity and precision. She has very high qualifications in her sphere and is intensely proud of her department and its skills. A new product has been developed by a rival company, and it is necessary to ascertain its structure as soon as possible.

3. Mark is a chief engineer specialising in tunnel design. He is a strong manager who rules his section with a rod of iron, but you suspect a heart of gold quietly hidden in his desk. A range of sites and methods are possible for a new tunnel between two islands. Mark is required to produce a range of tenders.

4. Marge is a market research co-ordinator and controls a team of some twenty interviewers. A client has plans for a new launch of a cosmetic and requires market information.

How would you brief the four people, all of whom are excellent at their jobs?

Indicate whether you would need to dwell on the *Why*, the *What* or the *How* of the job.

How would your supervision of their work differ from your briefing?

——————————▶

Looking at Max, the system architect, we see that his problem is primary motivation: his Natural Child needs to be stirred in some way so that his Adapted Child will allow him to get down to the job. He needs to have the cycle of *Now–Why–What–How* started, and understand *Why*. Directly contacting his Adapted Child, perhaps by coming at him with a Critical Parent, will be counter-productive. He needs to be taken into the first segment of the cycle of change by some emotional appeal – not excluding threats – and then to be supervised round the cycle once he begins. His strength is creativity, but the creativity needs to be guided to make sure it knows why it is required and perhaps, maybe later, how it is to be used – the creative person is always able to find dozens of other exciting things to do. Someone else would be well advised to take away from Max the engineering 'how' and 'if' questions of commercial application. This is where he needs to be supervised: he is an expert at the *Why* bit of the cycle and will resent interference. An *emotive* Natural Child to Natural Child could work, as could a *supportive* Nurturing Parent to Adapted Child:

'Come on Max, get your butt out of the seat and do it.'

or:

'Max, I'm a bit worried about the team. If they don't get your contribution soon . . .'

Mary, the analyst, is the specialist in *What* questions, and simply needs to be told 'why' she is needed. My earliest recollection of supplying samples to an analyst not that dissimilar to Mary is of him coming into my lab and saying:

'OK, I give up. What are they and what do you want? Sample 34b is no good to me.'

Mary needs supervision not over what she does, but how she does it. The *What* specialist will choose the best method for perfection, with no regard for applications unless these are closely defined. Here we would take the *logical* Adult to Adult approach:

'The Company needs to know the exact formulation so that we can prepare a patents strategy . . .'

Mark, the civil engineer, is the *How* specialist and needs to be given clear instructions on *What* is required of him and his team. *Directive* Critical Parent to Adult instructions are required:

'I need to have a costing of two possible tunnels from the mainland to the island. The first has to cover . . .'

I would supervise Mark on the consequences of his recommendations – the *If* questions.

Marge, the market researcher, is an Action Woman and needs to be told very clearly how the survey should to be conducted. She will get it done. Again *directive* instructions are required:

'The survey must cover a reasonable demographic split, but get the researchers to realise that time is of the essence. Basically the client is interested in people who will buy the product, so keep it down to a sample of 500 people between 20 and 45 . . .'

Giving directive Critical Parent to Adult instructions is not easy, I have found, for many people. It means taking responsibility, and as managers we are often afraid of the direct command and somehow slip, if not into apology, then into either the whine of the Adapted Child or an uncontrolled attempt at Critical Parent to the other's Adapted Child. The uncontrolled Critical Parent chooses to control the individual and not the task.

The *Why person* needs to be motivated, either by appealing to the Natural Child or the Nurturing Parent. Supervision is likely to be resented but certainly will have to cover the *What* area.

The *What person* needs to be joined in Adult and supervised in Directive Critical Parent to Adult, looking into the *How* issues of his or her work.

The *How person* needs to have the Adult satisfied by Critical Parent, and to be supervised by looking at the *If* consequences.

The *If person* needs to be given very clear instructions, often in Adult but occasionally in Natural Child or Nurturing Parent. He or she is inclined to rush at things and needs a very special form of management which will be dealt with in the later chapter on the roles of management.

In this chapter I have detailed a simple model that allows us to look at the manager–subordinate relationship in a dispassionate way. I have hinted at a useful classification of people, but I will leave the classification itself to a later chapter. In the next chapter, I will extend the discussion about answering the *Why* questions, but this time I will use the more honoured word, *motivation*.

CHAPTER FOUR

Motivating the Individual

'How do I motivate staff – I can't hire, fire, discipline, or even control rewards.'

'Our company provides sports facilities, medicare, pensions, the lot. It may get better people at interviews, but it certainly doesn't motivate existing people; they take it for granted.'

'My people have to do boring jobs – someone has to. They get bored.'

'The company does its best to make people belong, but who wants a gold watch these days?'

> . . . *He was married and added five children to the population,*
> *Which our Eugenist says was the right number for a parent of his generation,*
> *And our teachers report that he never interfered with their education.*
> *Was he free? Was he happy? The question is absurd:*
> *Had anything been wrong, we should certainly have heard.*

March 1939   W. H. Auden, 'The Unknown Citizen'

Motivation of people at work

If we were able to ignore the word 'motivation', life would be much simpler; but it is inescapable in any book about management.

I was discussing office automation with a manager responsible for customer records in a large organisation. As I worked through the changes and the problems they were likely to present, I began to ask *Why*? Why was he so set on spending considerable sums on an untried system when the present partially computerised system seemed to be working well? 'Well, it would be easier.' I pressed my 'why' question. 'Well, it would allow management more control.' I pressed further. 'Well, it would get rid of the people: machines only require the right plug and they keep going. I'm not very good with people.'

'Machines only require the right plug and they keep going' is the reason why so many companies, ranging from General Motors down to the smallest private busines, hurry to purchase robots and computers. To work effectively people require considerably more than being connected to the mains.

> 'I tell them what to do, give them the means to do it and in exchange I pay them money. A fair day's work for a fair day's pay is all I ask for.'

If only it were that simple. But fortunately for the writer of this book, people seem to want something extra – the intangible we summarise as 'motivation'. If this were not so, then the market for management books would vanish overnight.

The offices, factories, schools and shops of the manager's world fulfil two roles. Formally they provide products or services, and informally they provide some sort of social support for the people employed, managers and their staff. Both these roles are vital, interrelated and essential to an effective organisation. The question 'What motivates people?' has occupied many minds, from the workshop supervisor after a particularly frustrating Monday morning after the home team has lost, to the academic spending a life trying to develop a unified theory. In practice, the point that emerges is that the working process caters for a wide range of human needs, and that these needs are assembled into various unique packages for each individual at different stages in his or her working life. Accepting the uniqueness of the combination of factors for each individual, I think it is helpful for the manager to concentrate on areas where he or she has the time, the effort, the inclination *and* the control. Once you have established your constraints, or indeed the constraints forced upon you, you can decide how to act. You may find that your freedom to act is so small that you are unable to motivate your staff. You may find that your own motivation is so low, and your matches so damp, that you cannot even get to the blue touch-paper of motivation. I will enable you to reassess your position at various states in the book.

Put at its simplest, the answers to the question 'Why do people work?' can be placed under four general classifications. The first is the most obvious: *money* – survival for ourselves and our families. We work to provide ourselves with a means of trade which provides food and shelter to satisfy our physiological needs and, beyond them, a choice of lifestyle. The second is *belonging* – the society and companionship of others, and this is the principal subject of the next chapter. The third is *status or esteem* – we like to be able to identify a position within an order, within a pattern, and to use this position as a home base for exploration. It seems we all like to be able to answer the question 'What do you do?', and to feel secure with the answer. Those neat labels round our necks ('Anglo Foods – I'm a buyer') allow us to be accepted without awkward silences. They enable us to avoid the terror of being the only one unable to answer because we are 'resting' at the time.

Listening to the answers his workers give to the question 'What do you do?' may also give a perceptive manager some clues as to how they feel about the organisation.

George had worked well for a strong company within a multi-national and was being tested for 'higher things'. His test-bed was a company making consumer products which the organisation had acquired in Ireland. The factory was tatty and his primary analysis of the balance sheets confirmed his view that much needed to be done. The Irish company's position in the market-place was poor, the product line badly regarded, and the business strategy virtually non-existent. The company, though inefficient and apparently aimless, did have a reasonable team of second-level managers.

After a very hard first week and a particularly long day, George found himself in a local bar sampling the stout. He had no intention of spying on a group of his process operators in the next bar, but found it impossible not to eavesdrop. A newcomer came to the table and asked one of his shift supervisors where he worked. There was a slight hesitation: 'I'm on the docks.' George knew at that moment that what he had seen as a hard problem was going to be very difficult indeed.

The fourth motivation, for the fortunate, is concerned with *identification towards a task*. We, the fortunate ones, actually see something of ourselves in the progress or completion of the work in hand. We like to be associated with producing a particular product, solving a problem, working long hours to help the sick,

or even writing a book for new managers. Something happens and
we find ourselves saying:

> 'I'm lucky. I'd do this job even if they didn't pay me!' (I hope
> my publisher isn't listening, but as I said before, I enjoy my
> job.)

In the four classes of motivation there is a form of hierarchy, an
order in the factors that motivate us; but the pattern is by no
means simple – as you will see when we get down to detail. In the
'bad old days' of the Iron Rule in newly industrialised nineteenth-
century Britain, the reasons for working in the foundries, the
mines and the mills were simple and very often brutal. For the
great mass of workers, the prime motivation was escape from
grinding poverty and real starvation. Some of the owners of the
mills were even quoted as setting wages to provide sufficient for
survival plus a 'renewal' of the workforce. Remnants of this form
of extreme Critical Parent attitude can still be heard today when
people talk of attempting to limit coalminers' pay 'so that they will
have to come in for the Friday shifts'. I suspect that you, as a
manager well into the fourth quartile of the twentieth century, will
have to deal with workers whose expectations are concerned more
with lifestyle than with survival or even subsistence. Lifestyle is a
difficult master to satisfy.

However, let's look at the four areas of motivation from the
point of view of the actual constraints within which you work.
The mechanisms of monetary reward are unlikely to be available
to you unless you are managing your own company, and a small
one at that. National legislation, market forces, company policy,
unions, and similar factors outside your control – however just,
helpful and valuable in an overall sense – reduce your freedom of
action, increase your impotence. In an organisation of any size,
the most flexibility you can expect is your own input to the
company's wages/salaries review system, or perhaps the detail of
the bonus system. However, we must not be too naive and think
that we have to restrict the 'rewards' solely to money. Money can
be used by the individual to buy a better lifestyle, but it can also be
used by the employer to 'provide' a better lifestyle. Hours of
working and flexitime systems, holidays, canteen arrangements,
saunas, private medicine systems, new working equipment – all
affect the motivation of staff to the extent that they consider your
organisation offers a package that meets their aspirations better
than that offered by Henry Higgins down the road. They may
assist you in getting a better choice of worker, and they do not

have to be expensive. I know, for instance, of a manager of a clerical department who fought organisational parsimony over replacing ageing typewriters with reconditioned machines. By providing new and state-of-the-art machines he improved both morale and efficiency at minimal cost.

There are problems, however, in offering 'lifestyle' improvement. The first one is that of equity.

Grommet Packaging was a firm specialising in repacking products purchased in bulk, using small quality cartons and containers. Their skills were in the flexibility of their staff, who were mostly female, part-time and on weekly rates well below national averages. The women were able to fix their working days to fit personal commitments, and a bonus system allowed some increase of earnings.

As the firm expanded it found that the supply of plastic containers to the quality it demanded was restricted, and it decided to begin manufacture on site. The moulding machinery was very expensive relative to the re-packing lines and had to be operated on a three-shift, seven-day cycle. The process workers, mostly men, were recruited specifically for the job and were paid the industrial standard, some two to three times that of the packaging department part-timers. The process plant was in a connecting building to the packing plant and had a drinks vending machine.

When I went to the factory the maintenance men, who were based with the packers, had virtually refused to work in the process plant, and trouble was looming generally.

Before the arrival of the process plant workers, the part-time staff had been perfectly happy with their money and their lifestyles. What they told me now was that they wanted equal rewards. The problem for management was considerable. The process workers were difficult to recruit and were getting pay commensurate with the job. The packers' job was routine and they were getting paid accordingly, but this was not seen to be *fair*.

The next issue giving concern to management seeking to motivate by improving lifestyles is that the standards of lifestyle are changing *outside* the workplace. As the expectations of housing and leisure have increased, the cost of making workplaces desirable to work in has increased accordingly.

The third issue is that whatever you give in fringe benefits, today's become the expected norm for tomorrow – people get used to them and expect them as of right. Many fringe benefits can be seen as a management trap: they act as a disincentive if removed.

The fringe benefit of today becomes the 'as of right' factor of tomorrow, and management may need to spend many creative hours finding new fringe benefits to act as motivators. The cost of fringe benefits can well drag companies to the wall, and they are often the first things that employees lose when take-overs occur. I also know of several large companies saddled with sports and social clubs, regular inflation-proof salary reviews, medicare schemes and the like, who have deliberately set up wholly owned subsidiaries in new business areas with none of these costly additional trappings.

The creative manager of a new company needs to look for fringe benefits with the same eye as the skilled negotiator:

'What can I give that others value more than it costs me?'

A market survey company had a number of interviewers to whom they had given a period of training and whom they then used on an ad hoc, seasonal basis, as work demanded. To an outsider this would not seem a very attractive proposition, but they had found a formula that meant that they had an almost embarrassing response to their recruitment advertisements. They encouraged their part-time staff to slot their work in the most convenient way to meet their home commitments. As the company was also part of a much larger group, the part-time staff also saw the work as a convenient bridge across the 'family gap'.

The working arrangement cost the company nothing and its gain was considerable.

In my example of the new typewriters, the machines cost several hundred pounds, but weighed against the loss and replacement of a skilled secretary this was negligible – less than the cost of a single job advertisement.

The *belonging needs* of people at work will be the subject of much of the rest of the book. Here I would like you to accept that many of the jobs you control are not structured for human contact. People vary as to needs for social contact, ranging from the 'night watchman by choice' to the people-junky working in a holiday camp, but most people like company. The worker on a noisy flow line, the sole adult at a blackboard 'fighting' noisy teenagers and the assistant in a small store – all have limited social contact; but something can always be done, provided we accept the problem. The 'Music While You Work' principles developed in the Second World War do work to produce a camaraderie on the shop floor, and a decently organised staffroom relieves stress in schools.

Probably the most efficient retailing chain in Britain has regular coffee mornings where all the staff, by rota, meet with their managers and regional manager. New staff meet their colleagues and people share problems.

Cost to the company – virtually nil, since the regional manager would have to visit anyway and the day chosen is a slack one and easily covered by the remaining staff. Value to the company – immense. Value to the staff – well, they feel as if they belong to a working family and are valued, and that's good.

The *status and role security* aspects of motivating people to work may not be obvious areas where the New Manager can make an impact. The perception of jobs depends on the attitudes of many people. No matter how much a supervisor may explain the importance of the job of toilet cleaner and give it dignified job titles, ultimately the entire environment – people and things – will confirm the role and the status. But the confirmation does not always have to be negative.

The deputy managing director of a food manufacturing plant was on one of his walkabouts. The walkabouts were frequent and welcomed. A standard stopping-point in his visits was the staff washroom. On this occasion he followed the visit by going into the cleaners' hut and asking who was responsible for cleaning the A Block toilets. A rather surprised cleaner accepted responsibility and was asked why he thought his job was important in the plant. The cleaner answered that hygiene was necessary for all of them to keep their jobs, and hygiene started in the toilets – this was a company wall slogan. The director agreed. He then asked whether the A Block toilets gave any different problems from the others on site. The cleaner pointed out that the low-level flush tanks were not really man enough for the job. He understood that there was not enough space for the old-fashioned high-level versions, but 'they just aren't as good'.

The entire A Block toilets were converted back to high-level flushes, and the cleaner was acknowledged in the company staff suggestion-scheme awards.

The story of the cleaner is really about the manager acting as a 'housekeeper' for the most valuable resource of all – people. Management by Walking About involves just this, seeing, acknowledging, rewarding and admonishing so that everyone on the site has recognition. It does not mean just seeing the odd patch of oil spillage or hearing the noisy class. You, when you walk about the site, make sure that everyone has some territory he or she can call their own, that names are on lockers and that the keys work. You can make sure that your work-group has some claim to fame – the best safety record, the best-looking piece of beefcake, the champions at billiards or even the most militant shop steward in the group. There is always something that can be done to reduce the anonymity of your group.

The perception of your group by the rest of the organisation cannot be changed easily. Organisations seem to have attitudes, just as individuals have attitudes, and they look upon groups of workers, sections, departments, in very stereotyped and perhaps archaic ways. In a later chapter I shall detail some of the possible problems concerned with changing organisational perceptions. None of them is easy.

Before we go on to the last of our motivation classifications we need to remember that we, as managers, are also people who have needs – we do indeed bleed. Wendy Hirsh of the Institute of Manpower Studies in the UK gave an interview to the British *Sunday Times* in 1987 about the effects of fast-track or high-flyer schemes in large organisations. In these, potentially brilliant managers are identified at the point of departure from specialisation to becoming a New Manager. After that they are treated differently and coached for high office. She said:

'High-flyer schemes seep into the culture of any organisation and are bound to produce élitist beliefs about what kind of manager is valued. To understand the adverse effect this can have on company morale, you only have to put yourself in the shoes of a manager who knows his company operates a high-flyer scheme, and also knows he is not in it.'

Wendy Hirsh might be talking about our group of élite process workers and the part-time packing girls. Esteem is important to all of us.

The last motivation factor classification was concerned with *identification with the task* or as Maslow, a very distinguished worker in management behaviour put it, self-actualisation. Some of us are lucky enough to find ourselves and our jobs favourably intertwined, but even if we do, not having enough to eat could act as a considerable demotivator. Maslow saw the four motivating classifications in a strict hierarchy. He considered that each had to be satisfied before the next was sought or became important. He saw the first in the hierarchy was the need to satisfy physiological needs – food, shelter, survival of self and family. If these needs are not satisfied, a human being will devote all energies towards their satisfaction. I like to think of the hierarchy in terms of our cave-dwelling ancestors. Once they had a reasonable cave, a mate, a source of food and warmth, they began to think of creating tribes. Belonging to a tribe was important to the watered and fed caveman. Once belonging had been satisfied there was one's role, one's position in the tribe. One had to be recognised for something – cave painting, knowing the herbs, particularly frightening make-up, hunting mammoths – something that gave status. Once status had been achieved it was possible to think about being a craftsman. So it is with us. First of all we need a source of income; then we need to belong to some sort of organisation; and then we demand some role clarity. After that we can venture into the high-risk area of self-actualisation. Many of you, and more of your staff, will never achieve the clarity of role to allow you the luxury of self-actualisation, the very nature of the work precludes it. But we can do something.

The food manufacturer I discussed previously had problems of quality from some of its many plants throughout the UK. Looking at the packs that went to the customers you would see 'Bloggo Foods, Head Office London'. There was no mention of the fact that the product was made in Shipton-on-the-Sea or East Waring. The attitude was that if the quality was poor, then blame Head Office. There was no factory accountability. Why not?

Reorganisation of work can make it more stimulating, but it is necessary to find out whether this is a good idea. If the workforce, as in the case of our part-time packers, is being paid subsistence wages, who wants to be involved? The happy factory is not necessarily the most efficient: happiness and low costs are not necessarily co-runners.

I began this chapter by saying that you are unlikely to be able to control many of the motivation factors. Before we explore an area that you certainly *do* control, let's look at your opportunities and limitations.

-------►

EXERCISE

How much freedom do you have to motivate your staff?

Monetary Rewards

Do you have a say in what your subordinates are paid?

If you do, just how significant is your voice?

Is your subordinates' pay in any way related to effort, quality or quantity?

What/who determines pay rates –
> National union agreements?
> Local agreements?
> Market forces?
> Personnel department of your company?
> . . . . .?

Do you have any say in the 'conditions of service'?

Who sanctions changes in service conditions?

Belonging Rewards

Can you influence the quantity of group contact?

Can you influence the personal contact environments?

Do you think the amount of personal contact is sufficient?

Do your subordinates have contacts outside your section?

Status and Role Rewards

Outside, do your people have recognisable titles?

If there are menial role titles, can you alter this?

What sort of image has your group in the organisation?

Could you improve on your group's status?

Intrinsic Rewards of the Job

Is the nature of many of your subordinates' jobs boring, whatever may be attempted to change this?

How much latitude do you have in enriching jobs?

Are your people aware of company objectives?

Are there any objectives of the organisation or your group that could be seen as challenging?

In my experience a great many readers will find this checklist strangely depressing. Yes, you may find yourselves saying, there is very little that I can do – perhaps you are writing this book for the wrong person: all right – *What can I do*? There is a great deal the individual manager can do, and the language I shall use is taken again from Eric Berne.

The concept of personal appreciation in the workplace

One whole school of management theory, which I shall discuss later, has been nicknamed the 'Hello Dolly' system. At its beginning, this school encouraged supervisors to wander round a plant at start-up and say 'hello' to everyone on the shift. Empathically used, formally acknowledging people every day does improve morale and was one of the precursors of the 'Management by Walking About' system I have mentioned. The problem I have met with the 'Hello Dolly' method arises when a very Critical Parent manager, who may not recognise himself as such, attempts it. I went round a department with such a manager who greeted everyone as long lost brothers, or somehow as glamorous slave girls, and the effect was horrendous. If, when you acknowledge your staff, you have any feeling of talking down to them, do be careful and if possible get a trusted colleague to walk round with you. People notice being talked down to: they are looking out for it and they react badly when they find it.

When Berne developed his concept of Transactional Analysis – part of which I used in my discussion of states of mind – he also studied the way people need the acknowledgement of other human beings. He gave the name *stroke* to a unit of currency of acknowledgement, and he claimed that humans needs strokes to survive. Just as his work on states of mind could be related to the work of a neuro-surgeon, Dr Wilder Penfield, the origin of Berne's work on strokes lies with Spitz, a scientist working with children in US orphanages. Spitz demonstrated that children who were literally 'not touched' by others not only showed behavioural problems but also were under-size for their age. He also showed, quite amazingly at the time, that a regime of very high human contact, using a team of surrogate mothers, was able to restore normality. Berne made the intellectual leap that what could be demonstrated for children must at least have some validity for adults. There is some evidence now that Berne was correct, in that major disorders can be inflicted on prisoners who are deprived of *all* human touch in 'brainwashing' tanks. Recently it has been

acknowledged by those entrusted with the care of old people that
pets add comfort and prolong the life of their solitary owners.

I am not suggesting that, in industry, commerce and education,
efficiency would be improved if we all had hugging sessions at the
start of each day – the results could well include the effects of other
factors that might mask any improvement in working power.
What I am saying is:

PEOPLE NEED PEOPLE
WORK IS A MAJOR PART OF MANY PEOPLE'S LIVES
PEOPLE SEEK HUMAN CONTACT AT WORK
and
THEY WILL GET IT WITH OR WITHOUT YOU!

The 'units of human contact' – strokes – can come wholly from
other workers, and you may find yourself a stranger in your own
section. They may come wholly from the organisation's customers, and you will find your salesmen behaving as if they
worked for your customers and not you. Worst of all, they may
come from groups or individuals whom you mistrust as agitators
and then you will have real trouble.

> When a new large modern hospital was built for a growing city, the
> haematology unit was left some miles away in the grounds of what
> had been the old cottage hospital. Samples were sent to the
> haematology unit for test and returned in a number of vans. The
> only contact the manager of the unit had with the main building
> was at monthly meetings, and the only communications he and his
> workers received were complaints for defective work. The haema-
> tology unit became totally inward directed, inefficient and alien-
> ated from the hospital. More significantly perhaps, it became the
> centre of industrial action for the whole region.

People gravitate to where they are recognised and, in the case of
the haematology unit, this was towards agitators, who at least
recognised their presence. Berne's concept of strokes gives us a
language to discuss how this sort of phenomenon can and does
happen, and gives us a strong lead towards preventive action. It
shows how you as a manager can work more effectively by being
in control of the stroke pattern of your group.

▶

EXERCISE

I want you to look at your stroke pattern at work. Berne saw five types of stroke:

Unconditional Positive	You are valued as a human being and there is no price tag. You do not have to do anything to get an Unconditional Stroke: 'Its nice having you around.'
Conditional Positive	You have done something well and are told so: 'Well done.' 'Thank you for coming.' 'I like that dress.'
Conditional Negative	You have not done something and are told so: 'Those results are weak.' 'Your suit is shabby.' 'Get a job.'
Unconditional Negative	You are not valued as a human being and can do nothing right: 'Get out of my sight.' 'What do you expect from women/children/Catholics . . .'
Complete discount	Ignoring: '. . . in the next room' '. . . we may get some trouble from them but . . .'

Think of the last two weeks at work. Categorise and list the strokes you have received, you have given, and your section has given and received.

Do you feel good about what you have recorded? If not, what have you done to help yourself?

What do you suspect the others around you have done if they, too, feel bad –
>Taken it out on their spouses?
>Joined a union?
>Given an extra discount to a customer?
>Foul-mouthed the organisation?

When you look at your pattern at work, you may well find that the preponderance is towards negative conditionals – people tell you, and you tell others, of defects. Management by Exception is a management style which glorifies this preponderance as a route to efficiency:

> 'Look, you've done your job – that's what you're paid to do isn't it? I'll tell you when you get it wrong.'

Fine, but we do need to be told when we get it right as well. Blanchard and his co-writers in the series of books on the *One Minute Manager* explain the principle of sound motivation:

---

1. Give clear, monitorable and understood objectives.
2. Seek out, explain what you are doing and give immediate, short and succinct praise.
3. Recognise deficiencies, explain what you are doing and give immediate, short and succinct admonishment:
   Criticise the Behaviour and not the person.
   Be specific and only consider the avoidable.
   Say how you feel and how it affects you in your job.
   Give the person unconditional strokes.
   Close the matter for good.

The manager who praises good work honestly and admonishes poor behaviour in subordinates, peers or even bosses, clearly and frankly, does gain the respect and following of those around. However, people vary in their demands for strokes from management, and that is the subject of the next chapter.

CHAPTER FIVE

Different Strokes for Different Folks

'When I get home I just want to get a beer, put my feet up and watch the telly – anything. My wife wants to talk; I could kill her.'

'With promotion I just don't get any real time with the family.'

'I used to like the company get-togethers; now I find them embarrassing.'

'If only I could delegate more.'

'I do all this "hello" stuff to my staff, but some people seem to want it all the time.'

'I like people and especially my group, so when I give difficult orders and they turn their backs, I feel bad.'

In the last chapter I discussed 'the manager as motivator', finding ways that you could, given the real constraints of real organisations, motivate staff. We saw that the hierarchy of motivating factors – money and lifestyle, belonging, esteem and self-actualisation – could offer you some ways of improving staff performance, but that the simple concept of giving appropriate personal recognition probably offered more opportunities. In this chapter I am going to extend the concept of personal recognition – strokes – to show how both the quality and the quantity of strokes required vary with individuals. I am proposing that, by understanding the quality of strokes you and your staff demand, you may be able to plan your working, private and leisure life more effectively. I am also proposing that, by recognising the variety of individual requirements as to the volume and nature of strokes, you will be able to understand your own interactions with groups (the actual dynamics of groups will be tackled in the next chapter).

-----------→

EXERCISE

Imagine you are listening to a speech in your honour.

Make a list of the things you would like to hear, and put them down in order of importance to you.

Think of the various people who might be giving the speech. How would this affect your list, and how you would feel about the whole occasion?

What sort of 'state of mind' in the speech-giver would you prefer?

Go back to your list of 'strengths and weaknesses' from Chapter 1 and remember how I asked you to classify them in terms of whether you would:

1. be happy for them to be public knowledge;
2. prefer them to have only a limited circulation; or
3. prefer them to remain hidden except in very special circumstances.

How does what you want to hear fit this classification?

Imagine that the speech-giver makes certain mistakes of fact or opinion. Is the effect on you related to your classification?

-----------►

I am very aware of the pitfalls of making eulogistic speeches about working associates but, when forced, I attempt to maintain a ritualistic approach. The blatantly untrue in the form of old jokes is my retreat. I maintain the entire presentation in the recipient's 'public knowledge' sector, with little teases into the 'limited circulation' sector. I have even been known to say the magic words:

'Now that it is appropriate, I'd better let you into a secret about Bloggs . . .'

My 'state of mind' is at best Little Professor, and my frequent slips into Natural Child are probably the reason why I am seldom asked to do the job. I have to know the recipient very well, and the audience has to be very select indeed, for me to depart from this ritual. Imagine just such an occasion – the presentation of a gold watch for fifteen years' service to Bloggs Engineering:

> 'I would like you all to welcome Roger Ackroyd. Roger has been with the company for fifteen years and foreman supervisor of the maintenance section for the last ten. During that period he has instilled a spirit of quality and service that is second to none.
>
> 'Roger is of course a Yorkshireman of renown who, though qualified to play cricket for the county, hasn't had much success in games I've seen. Roger is of course married and has two lovely boys, both of whom I hope will follow their father's footsteps into the old firm.
>
> 'The gold watch . . .'

The speaker is happily and safely into ritual when he reads out the material about Roger from the company's personnel records. Roger has had that amount of service and has had that job. We can imagine Roger warming to the occasion and the recognition on a public scale that he exists. He is being stroked positively, in front of a lot of people, for things that he has done. His pleasure will very likely increase when the speaker – moving from the ritual into description of the work itself – strokes him about the way he does the job. The praise is probably taken from Personnel records, but perhaps it could mean that the speaker has actually taken an interest. The appropriate disclosure is pleasant. The Yorkshire joke is old and certainly the sort of thing that anyone with an accent has to bear, but it leads on to something else. Suppose Roger did not discuss his family in public and it was part of his 'hidden' area. Suppose what was 'public knowledge' about the size and sex of his family did not represent the whole truth. Suppose one of his boys was giving him and his wife intense problems, and the chances of the boy joining the firm were non-existent. How would Roger feel? We have moved into Roger's 'hidden' area with the associated gain of a large stroke *if correct*, and the associated risks if even fractionally wrong. There is a hierarchy of strokes, just as there is a hierarchy of motivational needs. In the hierarchy of strokes the risk increases with the opportunity.

Ritualistic strokes about the 'public knowledge' sector of our lives are fine; and the very acknowledgement of our existence to an audience makes us feel good, and public recognition from a respected or senior person in our lives makes us feel even better. Strokes about our way of working are worth more to us, but there is more risk. One of Roger's engineers might have been present and given a cough of disapproval when he or she heard the compliment. Strokes to our 'hidden' area – intimate strokes – have a very high value indeed, but carry a proportionate risk.

Berne, from whom I derived my discussion of states of mind, considers that we all adopt a strategy for obtaining strokes, and structure our lives accordingly. Our strategy is to divide our time in such a way as to achieve a certain weight of strokes – a lot of low-value strokes at low risk or a few high-value strokes at high risk, to make up our quota. The way he sees us structuring our time is in terms of the following:

Definition		Risk	Value
Withdrawal	– away from people completely	Very low	Very low
Rituals	– highly structured contact	Low	Low
Procedures	– formalised contacts	Low/Medium	Medium
Activities	– informal with high task	Medium/High	Medium
Pastiming	– social contact with rules	Medium	Medium
Intimacy/ Games	– informal meetings of a people kind	Very high	Very high

Withdrawal is the time when we get away from people completely, either physically or in the mind. Withdrawal can sometimes be a rational decision when one needs to 'recharge one's batteries', to be alone and away from people pressures for a perhaps brief time. One manager recently described withdrawal as the manager's decompression chamber. Or, according to Berne's concept, it is a way of restoring the balance of people contacts to the level chosen and required by the Adult. Withdrawal can, in inappropriate circumstances, be sulking, a way to avoid unpleasantness, rows or simply things we do not approve of, and do not have the motivation to tackle effectively. Sometimes this form of physical sulking, coming from our Adapted Child, takes the form of actually leaving the scene; but more often it is simply 'turning off', regardless of the potential human contacts around. In any long meeting, it is almost certain that at least one person is 'not really there' and has withdrawn in all but physical presence.

You can recognise whether your own behaviour at a particular time is withdrawal or not by thinking of what happens when you are disturbed. A person working alone may welcome a cup of coffee, but the person who is withdrawing will regard even a well-intentioned cup of coffee as an intrusion. I know of many people in the 'people business' – trainers, salespersons, entertainers – who need the 'decompression chamber' before they return home to meet the world. For them the journey home is withdrawal, and they would no more pick up a hiker or talk to a stranger than fly.

Some jobs in your organisations demand a level of privacy, and seeking this out can be mistaken for deliberate withdrawal. As you, the New Manager, progress up the tree, the need for such periods will increase, and a wise organisation organises peer-group contact. We all need to withdraw sometimes at work, but withdrawal for extended periods is not good for the individual or the organisation. As the producer of this book, I recognise that writing is a lonely activity, and I find myself suddenly deciding that I have had enough and wander about with the aim of talking to somebody – a stranger will do very well. You will need to do this as a manager, and will find a new reason for 'Managing by Walking About' – it could be the relief valve of the 'decompression chamber'.

The opposite is also true. If workers cannot get away from people sometimes, they become saturated with contacts, and sensible individuals and organisations provide areas of quiet. I know of companies who provide small cells in quiet parts of the building whose only access is by a centrally held key. Far from being used for sleep, the rooms act as 'decompression chambers' and have significantly lowered work-related dysfunctional stress, and improved the standards of creativity.

Rituals come in all shapes and sizes, from Royal Weddings to our formalised ways of greeting and parting with acquaintances. They are safe and helpful and save us from having to be original in the light of variations in common situations. In organisations they allow safe contact between individuals who have different interests and views but a common culture – that of the organisation itself.

Most organisations accept that some form of social mixing and enforced meeting between people from the whole range of the workforce is necessary. The organisations accept this but also choose to operate their social mixing – their distribution of mass strokes – at a safe and formalised level. Rituals are set up so that the rules are clearly understood by everyone taking part.

Stevens Foundries had been a family business and retained many of the traditions, one such being the annual dinner dance. Coaches picked up staff at time-honoured points throughout the area and arrived at the hall, where the directors and their wives were waiting, at precisely 20.00. As folk came through the door, each employee was formally welcomed and pointed towards 'the reception' and its choice of sweet or dry sherry from a starched and cleaned version of one of the canteen ladies. At exactly 20.30, dinner was announced and everyone sat down according to a precise seating plan. All middle and senior management staff had a long-serving member of Stevens Foundries and partner attached to their table – a conversational guide had been circulated previously. Dinner ended at 21.30 and the Chairman spoke: '. . . without whose untiring efforts this company would not exist . . .' and 'It is now my proud pleasure to present . . .' Gold watches and services of cutlery were presented and the managers on each table spoke a few further words to the recipient as they sat down blushing and happy. Dancing started at 22.15 and the coaches arrived to take people home at 23.30.

It worked very well until the company got into financial trouble, with its attendant redundancies. The Ritual ceased to be a source of positive strokes and as one workman put it when a 65-year-old sat down: 'If that old fool had retired when he could have done, maybe we could have taken on some kids this year.'

The Ritual had outlived its useful life and was stopped the next year.

The speech from the Chairman of Stevens Foundries would have been entirely in Ritual, and under no circumstances would he have taken any risk and discussed anything outside the 'public knowledge' area – nothing was ever said about the *man*.

The strokes from Ritual are real, and the pleasant feelings they produce are real, too. The problem of Ritual as a method of motivation by means of strokes lies in the shallowness of the strokes and the very stylisation which, of necessity, handicaps its ability to respond to change: the Chairman's address and the annual dinner dance were ideal within a static environment, but dangerous at a time of change. Once it is know that the company is in trouble and jobs are in jeopardy, a Ritual from a different past will misfire; and if the Ritual has become an assured 'right', its removal will be noticed and draw publicity to the problems.

Regular Monday morning meetings, Wednesday tours of the factory, by the board, Christmas parties for the office, Nativity plays – all may become Ritual and, as times change, may have ceased in their prime objective. *Rituals need to be reviewed regularly and in particular with changing circumstances.*

Procedures are formalised or understood ways of doing things.

Unlike Rituals they are subject to change, modification or review against a changing world of people and events, and without major formality.

'As MD I have an open door policy, and my secretary will be glad to fix up an appointment.'

The Procedure is a little more flexible than the Ritual, but still has a safety net available. The MD is visible, but only between certain hours and after a particular sequence has been observed. Prior notice ensures that the MD is prepared and, should political considerations appear, the meeting will not take place: although his door is always open, he will not be behind it. For the New Manager the very appearance of informality in the Procedures is a trap. 'We have ways of doing things in this department' is fine if you happen to know what the ways are. Some companies attempt to provide some procedural guidelines, while others have the attitude of keeping quiet until you go wrong. Procedures allow you to delegate – but more of that later.

The direct advantage of the Procedure over the Ritual is that it is less formalised and therefore more flexible, or should be. Unreviewed procedures can easily become Rituals, and bad Rituals at that. There is a British Army story about the spare man standing alongside a modern field gun doing precisely nothing. On looking into the Army procedures of the past, it was found that the man used to be required to calm the horses when the gun went off; but the horses had vanished in 1919 and it was now 1960.

Procedures speed human activities by reducing the opportunity for human error, but allow some individuality and hence a feeling of belonging and an accompanying sense of satisfaction beyond that provided by Rituals. The conversion of many working activities to Procedures – the flowline is a supreme example – has reduced the human contact of the workplace. The intention was to make the activities less risky, but since people still need human contact, the risk has often shifted a dimension. Disputes between craftsmen over the job have been replaced by more general disputes between management and workers.

Activities are often thought of as *work* – doing things we are skilled at, need to do or have done, in a way determined by the circumstances and not by tradition and rules. But to Berne they mean much more. Work, though we may dismiss it, is a wonderful way of developing social contact. Examples of Activities may include organising and running a meeting, working in a task-force, building a sand-castle . . . The structure of the task is left to individual discretion and controlled by the skills of co-workers and by convenience. Because the task controls at least part of the activity, the risk is reduced. Because human agreement is necessary for success, the rewards are great. However, the risks are still massive, and it is not too much of a joke to say that more acquaintances learn to hate each other than become friends through having to work together. I heard of one marriage guidance counsellor who recommended couples who could not decide on their future to wallpaper a room together. The joint-task would either cement or completely destroy what was left of their relationship.

Pastimes are literally ways of passing time with other people, talking about innocuous subjects or enjoying the mutual exchange of prejudice. We share a conversation in Parent, and one of the most obvious male topics is cars:

'What are you driving now?'

'A Heartibeast Mark 2, dynamic!'

'I thought the acceleration was giving trouble from nought to sixty.'

'It was, but with a Cramit Two injector, it works by . . .'

The participants in Pastimes choose their partners in such a way as to minimise the risk: they make as sure as possible that they are among people who share the same Parent concepts and avoid, in the example above, the chance of talking to a conservationist who objects to fuel-guzzlers in general. They also get a strong belonging-buzz of strokes from excluding others – women, for example, may talk about 'female' issues, and men about 'male' things. Such conversation really does exclude others: try joining in a 'male' or 'female' example of Pastiming from the other side and breaking the sex stereotyping – it isn't easy. At best you will stop the game; at worst you will be snubbed very badly indeed.

Intimacy is where there is a genuine exchange of feelings between people, usually on a one-to-one basis. Warmth, empathy, closeness or real affection is shared, perhaps through some mutual experience of working together in an Activity, or more possibly from the growth of a Nurturing Parent/Adapted Child relationship into something more.

Games are also usually on a one-to-one basis and may well, to the outsider, seem like Intimacy. They are *played* by people in accordance with psychological rules, as opposed to Intimacy with its open structure. In Games each player has to take a role – the Victim, the Rescuer, the Persecutor – rather like characters in a soap opera. In Intimacy the people taking part live in real life, and are not stereotyped into the good, the bad and the ugly.

Games and Intimacy provide the highest rewards of human contact: the stroke value is high, but the risk is high too. The feeling that one has dropped all pretence and shared one's 'hidden' area with another person is superb; but then the feeling of betrayal if it goes wrong . . .

Games provide a way of getting counterfeit high-value strokes, which is a lot better than getting no high-value strokes at all. The ambitious manager may draw attention to him- or herself by admitting to weaknesses that do not exist but somehow allow a threatened boss to show a more human face. The clerk may find it is difficult to get praise for work adequately done and therefore choose to 'help' everyone else in the office. He or she may rescue everyone else until you, the boss, find that the clerk's own work is inadequately done; and then you find yourself persecuting. You are forced into the persecutor role and the clerk gets a lot of notice, a lot of human contact, a lot of counterfeit strokes.

People want to be valued, to be noticed – they want attention. The flowline operator who gets no human rewards from management will find an agitator to fill the gap. The salesman who is given no recognition for real effort or even good sales figures, and is only told to increase targets, will 'join the customers'. The clerk who is ignored for doing the job will find jobs that do get notice.

You get what you stroke. If you only notice people when they fail and failure means special attention, of whatever kind, people will tend to fail. Remember the part-time packers and the process workers. The process workers were getting all the attention, but not any more . . . People are complicated; machines were never like this.

------------▶

EXERCISE

I would like you to draw up two pie charts of the way you see your life divided – one for work and one for home. Make the areas in the charts correspond to my headings: Withdrawal (W), Rituals (R), Procedures (PR), Activities (A), Pastimes

(PA), and Intimacy/Games (IG). Here is an example:

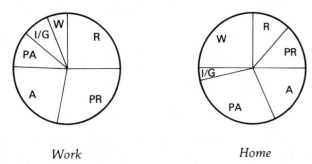

Work   *Home*

When you compare your charts a pattern may emerge.

The first chart is of a very senior manager and the high Ritual content is a result of public life responsibilities and of being a virtual figurehead for the organisation on many occasions. The senior manager gives out gold watches. Most of the response to organisational pressure have become Procedures, but there is space for Activities: there is a working party here and a working party there – with the Group, and working with other executives in a reorganisation plan, and one with Government representatives discussing public responsibility in the industry. The strokes from these Activities provide a great deal of job satisfaction, and compensate for some of the working skills he was able to use as a bench chemist before promotion to high office. There is not much time for Pastimes, but Games are part of the corporate culture.

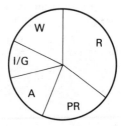

He is lucky in his choice of private secretary and executive team, all of whom provide Intimacy within the work situation. Withdrawal happens in trains and cars and planes. 'Executive class' is used to avoid fellow men and to 'recharge one's batteries' – true Withdrawal.

As a bench chemist our senior manager would have a pie chart something like this:

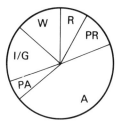

The chart is again balanced, with a considerable reduction in Rituals and a large increase in Activities. Intimacy is still quite high.

The change for the specialist with a high Activity content to their day, with its rich stroke rewards, to a day with a high and leaner Ritual content, is a likely feature of any New Manager's promotion. The effect may well be reflected first in home life, where more 'support' – or in our language, Nurturing Parent and possibly Intimacy – is required to maintain equilibrium. If the New Manager also wants the decompression chamber of withdrawal, then . . .

The next pie chart is of another senior manager.

Westbrown Holdings was a medium-size firm working in Public Relations and Advertising. Jane Brown left the organisation soon after its foundation, but John West remained at the head. He was truly proud of its growth and of the fact that he had hand-picked all the staff. He was a charismatic figure who chose to understand all the accounts and attend every presentation. He would say: 'When you think you are going to get an account, call me on the bleeper and arrange the meeting in an airport for twelve. There is nowhere in Europe you cannot get to by twelve and get back that evening – I like to be in my own bed – hate hotels.'

At work John West looked something like this:

He had virtually eliminated the possibility of Withdrawal at work – it was all done travelling. His meetings and discussions were at best Procedural and at worst interfering Ritual with a large Pastime and Game content. His inability to trust others lost him all chance of Intimacy with his managers, and was largely confined to tea ladies and other junior staff. At home he would have liked about fifty/fifty Withdrawal and Intimacy, but what he got was different. His Withdrawal was absolute: once home from airports and motor-ways, he would either go direct to bed or curl up by himself with a whisky and a book. The family learnt to go their own ways, and he found that Intimacy was very rare indeed – Games took their place. Rituals of the occasional family event remained, but otherwise he confined his Activities and Pastimes to the golf club and the bar.

Look at your old and new pie charts and think about the balances between your home and your work. Think about your new patterns in terms of the readjustments that the people around you – and in particular at home – may have thrust against them if they still want to keep contact with you. If your balance of stroke-demand between work and home is very biased, *over the long run* are you asking too much of either your private relations or your work? Only you know what you want and what you are willing to pay for it. Look, too, at your pie charts in terms of delegation. The areas you have desig-nated as Procedures are likely to be the best places to look for items that you can delegate. Rituals may annoy you, but they could well be your power base. They have a high profile and often provide the way you are judged by your own bosses.

'People need people' vs 'I do it my way' – the shoot-out

It is quite obvious that some people at work wither and die unless they have people around them: they need people *en masse*, they need to belong, they need to organise people and they need strong personal relationships and to get involved. Others are at the other end of the spectrum and simply go to work to do a job – the people around are incidental and often get in the way. Most of us lie between these two extremes.

————▶

EXERCISE

Give a total of ten marks to each set of questions, allocated as you see fit. Thus Question 1 could be (a) 3, (b) 0, (c) 2, (d) 5 = total 10.

Question 1
When you arrive at the office, do you:
(a) want to get straight down to work?
(b) find out what everyone has been doing the previous day?
(c) check up whether your instructions have been carried out?
(d) have an informal chat with a lieutenant?

Question 2
When you are invited to a firm's party, do you:
(a) think it's part of the job, but hope you are overseas at the time?
(b) look forward to it?
(c) remember you are organising it anyway?
(d) look forward to meeting some old mates?

Question 3
When you start working in a large group, do you:
(a) get into a corner and start work while they argue?
(b) worry whether you actually belong?
(c) get down to restoring order from the people chaos, or try to find out what role you are to play?
(d) look round for friendly faces?

Question 4
When you have to work away from base, do you:
(a) hope that they follow your clear instructions?
(b) feel that you may be left out of it on return?
(c) Make regular checks to see that they are on course?
(d) delegate to a lieutenant and exchange phone calls?

Question 5
If invited to present your work to a conference, do you:

(a) concentrate on the written presentation?
(b) get most concerned with the oral presentation?
(c) get involved with the organisation?
(d) look forward to the discussions after formal work?
The totals should add up to 50.
Your (a) total is _____
Your (b) total is _____
(c) total is _____
(d) total is _____   Total of (b) + (c) + (d) _____

The questions under (a) were concerned with the Task and ignored the people factors. The people factors were:

(b) *Joining and Belonging* needs – whether you regard being part of the group as important.

(c) *Role and Control* needs – your hierarchical and order concerns.

(d) *Pairing and Sharing* needs – the necessity for close human bonds.

If you have a higher (a) total than the total of (b) + (c) + (d) then you are not at work primarily for human contact: you want to get the job done. The lower your total (a) + (b) + (c), the lower your own stroke needs: you will probably be able to survive on a lean stroke diet – a bias towards Withdrawal and Rituals. The converse is true: the higher your (a) + (b) + (c), the greater your stroke needs and the more pressure you will be under if you cannot avoid a high proportion of Withdrawal and Rituals.

Let's look first at (b) – the Joining and Belonging needs. Many people make a Public claim to having large Joining and Belonging needs, and hide the fact that this is not true. The majority of managers I know do not like people *en masse* and would much rather do their own thing.

'I have been with this firm for ten years and each time I get invited to the Christmas thrash. Always I say 'Love to', but this is the first year I have not managed to be out of the country. I hate them. It's bad enough to have to work with people, without having to spend your private time with them as well.'

If you, as a manager, have high Belonging needs, or bring to the job the knowledge that you have high Belonging needs, then you are open to blackmail by the group that you manage. The threat of expulsion from the group will hang over you:

Henry was a warehouse manager and 'one of the boys', priding himself on having no 'them and us' attitudes, and enjoying a sociable pint after hours. He was an effective manager in that his schedules were always met and he had no labour disputes. He had worked his way up from the shop-floor and spoke rough. One night in the pub he was asked about redundancies in the rest of the firm and he promised, 'None of our our lot, over my dead body.' The next week he had to put in a forced redundancy scheme for 30% of his staff. I met him in therapy.

The higher your (c) totals, the more you are concerned with order, status, role, hierarchy and the control of people. It is perfectly acceptable to be concerned with all of these matters; but if they concern you a lot, you may find that they interfere with your task as a manager. You may find yourself acting inappropriately simply to satisfy some of these stroke needs, and consequently find yourself in trouble. I would suspect that you also had a high Critical Parent and a very strong set of standards.

The higher the (d) totals, the more you enjoy strong, intimate human contact at work. Again, as with high Joining and Belonging needs, there is a plus and minus. A high need for Pairing and Sharing can make it very hard to be tough in disciplinary situations. You may be seen as someone who can always be got around. The easy task may become difficult because nobody takes your decisions as final.

Most people do need the companionship of work – the strokes; but I do meet the occasional manager to whom people are merely tools. Then perhaps I move out of my roles and feel sorry for both them and those with whom they have to work.

Understanding your own various stroke needs and demands may help you to work more effectively, but the next chapter will explain how understanding the stroke needs and demands of others is an essential for effective management of teams. I will also look at the way teams develop, and at the roles necessary for an effective team.

CHAPTER SIX

Working with Groups and in Teams

'How the hell do you get them down to work in the morning?
They just seem to want to natter.'

'I need to get on with the job, but so much seems to be going
on they don't hear me.'

'This organisation . . . it's all covering up for mistakes,
blame and recriminations.'

In the last chapter I considered the planning of our lives so that we
receive our own personal quota of human contact, and the fact
that, since work is a major part of most of our lives, this factor
bears heavily on the way we behave at work. Some people need a
lot of human contact – strokes – and others less. I also found that
the human contact could be divided into three categories:

Joining and Belonging – the need for group contact

Role and Control – the need to have a clear role or control of
others

Pairing and Sharing – the need for individual contacts on a one-
to-one basis

The total of needs for human contact and their distribution vary
from individual to individual.

In this chapter I shall consider the effect of combining individuals into a group, and the way this combining of individual needs
forms a pattern in human behaviour. In a further chapter I shall
look at ways of improving team performance, including role
'engineering'.

Enough has been written for us all to understand that individuals vary. Put enough of us together in a group and we shall have
some people with negligible human contact needs and some who
might be described as 'people junkies', while the rest of us are
somewhere in the middle. In any group, there will be a distribution

of the forms of 'human contact' needs, and we shall have people with high Joining and Belonging needs, others with high Role and Control needs, and some with high Pairing and Sharing needs. Put all these people together and every kind of need has to be satisfied for somebody in the group before useful work can be accomplished. *The Joining and Belonging, Role and Control, Pairing and Sharing needs of a group have all got to be met before the group functions effectively.*

Imagine the situation where we meet somebody at a party. The first conversation is likely to establish whether, on the most global scale, we have the same set of prejudices. We have a Parent to Parent exchange:

'What do you think about the food? I like a bit of meat, myself.'

'Not a lot, and the people are a bit boring as well.'

'Did you see that man in the corner . . .?'

It has been established that we have the same set of prejudices; but if the response had been:

'I like vegetarian food, myself'

we might well have chosen to move on and try talking to somebody else so as to have no bones broken.

When we have found an individual or small group that relates to our set of prejudices, and it seems likely that we shall have our Joining and Belonging needs satisfied in the relationship, we can continue and find out whether our Role and Control needs are likely to be met:

'How about moving on?'

'I haven't got any transport.'

'Thats OK, I've got the firm's car.'

'Are you OK to drive?'

We have now established our roles – as respectively the 'driver and provider' and the 'caring and dependent' one, and it feels good. Again we have tested the water, and if we had not liked the roles that the potential relationship was likely to demand, we would probably have moved on again and tried elsewhere. But when we do feel that we are happy with the blooming relationship, we can start to develop towards real exchanges of confidences and Intimacy, to satisfy our Caring and Sharing needs:

'I'm not too happy at that sort of thing anyway.'

'Yes, the whole excitement of all those people frightens me as well.'

Other more task-orientated people might skip the preliminary stages and get directly down to Intimacy – the less obvious but more annoying kind being to bore you with details of their private history and feelings before you have even allowed them to get to know you. I am not saying that we consciously begin every relationship in this way, laboriously going through three distinct stages. What I am saying is that in growing to our mighty ages we have learnt certain social skills that, on the whole, stop us getting hurt and provide us with our people needs. Every time we succeed and meet these needs, the behaviour pattern is reinforced; and when we fail, we have an opportunity for refinement.

The stages of any human communication are in a set order:

Are we on the same lines – can we Join, do we Belong?

Can we establish ways of working together – have we a Role and who has Control?

Can we exchange Intimacy – do we have Pairing and can we Share?

Any group of people is likely to begin to go through the same stages every time it meets: a good example is the typing pool first thing in the morning. The Belonging issues may be passed through quickly on most occasions, but the slight movement of a desk will bring them to the fore, as will anyone returning from a holiday or from sick leave – 'What's happened when I was away, and do I still belong?' The group will also need to check out any events that have occurred since it last met which may have changed the balance of power or the roles of individuals. An urgent job may have been given to the typist last out of the office, and not to the one highest in the pecking order; or a new machine's arrival may mean a revised procedure. When, and only when, such issues are settled can the more intimate Pairing and Sharing – communication between close contacts – take place, and the group then get down to work willingly. The manager who tries to get work out of the typing pool before the sequence of events has been completed is in for a shock. The issue is not that the typing pool is unmotivated to work: it is simply that, the human needs have to be dealt with before effective work can happen. The sequence:

JOINING AND BELONGING NEEDS
ROLE AND CONTROL NEEDS
PAIRING AND SHARING NEEDS

is followed every day before *self-directed* work can happen.

It is possible for the manager to short-circuit the sequence, but then he or she has to direct the work completely. The group is not ready, and the responsibility for getting down to work and the task at hand is not shared. The manager with particular problems is the manager who has a strong task need and a low human contact need. He or she does not honour any of the stages, and is inclined to impatience when the more stroke-demanding dawdle through the stages when they are supposed to be getting down to work. Most of the managers reading this book are likely to have a low need in at least one of the three stages, and this could be the reason why they were promoted in the first place: proportionately high application to task is rewarded in most organisations. The manager with low Joining and Belonging needs may ignore the niceties of name badges and staff birthdays. The manager with low Role and Control needs may pass jobs betwen members of staff and ignore status and local hierarchy in communications. The manager with low Pairing and Sharing needs may well move staff without due consideration for friendships. As I have said already, it is possible to short-circuit the stages of development of the group on a daily basis, and certainly strong and firm management will help, as will effective communication of the urgency of the task. However, for easy and effective management it is probably better to accept the inevitable and use the stages to your own advantage. What can be ignored on a given day cannot be ignored over a long period. We can postpone Belonging needs and tell people they belong, we can postpone Role and Control needs and make up tight hierarchies with ourselves taking total responsibility, we can delay the formation of Pairing and Sharing by imposing a rush, but in time the human issues will catch up on us. On the whole, it is best to assume that the people around you need human contact, and that all the stages have to be followed on a daily basis. In my experience, people at work do wish to accomplish the task to the best of their abilities, but their priorities are unlikely to be the same as yours.

▶

EXERCISE

Look at your scores in the exercise on page 73 of the last chapter. In the light of what I have just discussed, are the scores under the headings of 'Task', 'Joining and Belonging', 'Role and Control' and 'Pairing and Sharing' recognisable to you, and do they fit the way you relate the *Task* to the *Process* content of your job? If not, go back to the questionnaire and check it out. (A number of very effective psychometric tests, including Schultz' FIRO B, give a much more reliable analysis of individual patterns of stroke demand, although the reader will find that the language in this book does not exactly fit that used by other authors.)

In terms of working with your section or department, is there any likely problem?

Have you noticed management problems that could be put down to your ignoring needs of one kind or another?

What steps can you take to improve the efficiency of your group by accepting that the needs will have to be satisfied on a daily basis?

▶

I have hinted that the daily stages of the development of a group are not the only issue that a New Manager needs to understand. In fact, the daily cycle is only a flicker in a much more important cycle. We can find ourselves in a group stuck in the Joining and Belonging stage for months or even years. Equally, and perhaps more unpleasantly, we can have a group stuck in the Role and Control stage, and life seems rather like a Borgias' tea-party. We may be lucky enough to be with a team working through the Pairing and Sharing stage, or even to have experienced working in a fully mature team where basic human relations were secure and subject only to the daily flicker.

Before I describe the 'symptoms' of living through teams in the four stages, I should like to digress and explain that some writers see the four stages in terms of 'ages of man' – the ultimate cycle for all of us. They see the stages as a way of explaining our personal life story and its problems. It is possible to see Joining and Belonging needs as the problems of childhood – are we wanted by the world and, in particular, our parents? If our Joining and

Belonging needs are not satisfied, we remain disturbed all our lives and never really get down to living. In adolescence, we concentrate on Role and Control needs – a statement that any parent of teenagers will bear witness to. Again, if these needs are not resolved to our personal satisfaction, we will not progress and will remain awkward for all of life. If Role and Control are resolved, the lucky parent and offspring then reach the Pairing and Sharing needs, which can be satisfied inside or outside the family. The jealousies of siblings will be replaced by respect and trust, and marriage could well be a relationship of mutual respect between equals. The successful life of just 'getting on with it' begins to decline with age, and the Pairing and Sharing may well lose ground as contemporaries die. The Role and Control issues rear their heads with old age, and the ultimate question could well be 'Am I alive or dead?' This is a Belonging issue to end all Belonging issues.

As managers, we are probably not greatly concerned with individual life-story issues, but we are concerned with the stages that groups, teams and organisations go through. I see recognising the symptoms or classical behaviours of each stage as being only the first step. If, in reading the next section of this chapter, you recognise that 'on the whole' your group has reached a particular stage, then think whether this is satisfactory. If it is not satisfactory, then what needs to be done can be discussed. Do not expect each and every symptom to occur in your own group, team or organisation: just look for the main flavour. I would also like you to remember that the stages are inevitable in the formation of any group and that, although some of the stages are distinctly uncomfortable even for the skilled manager, they are at worst lived through and at best accelerated.

---------►

EXERCISE

Imagine four teams.

In the first *undeveloped* team, the group is tackling Joining and Belonging needs. It is also avoiding any Role and Control issues, although some experimentation may occur. It certainly cannot deal with any individual Pairing and Sharing needs.

In the second *developing* team, more mature than the first, we are tackling the Role and Control issues, having settled the

Joining and Belonging ones. There may be some experimentation into Pairing and Sharing, but not a great deal.

In the third *consolidating* team, the majority of the Role and Control issues have been settled and we are moving into Pairing and Sharing. There are no concerns, other than on an ephemeral basis, to do with Joining and Belonging.

The final *mature* team has achieved a group and individual balance of human needs, and is performing without individual struggle.

How would the behaviour of the four teams differ to the outsider?
How would it feel to be working in each of the teams?
Do you recognise some of the behaviours from your own team and, if so, place it in one of the four categories:

> Undeveloped
> Developing
> Consolidating
> Mature

---------------------►

Stage 1 – Joining and Belonging: the undeveloped team

What the individuals in the group are attempting:

To discover the nature and boundaries of the task.

To find out and to test whether they personally are needed, and to delay any progress until they feel they are.

The behaviours a fly on the wall will observe:

Grumbling about the immediate conditions.

Intellectualising and talk about irrelevant issues.

Swift but uncommitted attempts to structure the group, define the task, get on with the job.

Mutual exchange of information and one-sided attempts to define positions.

Test of relations within the group, and temporary groupings

between obviously similar people – males/females, whites/ blacks, engineers/scientists.

Suspicion and wall-building.

Reliance on external leadership.

AN OUTSIDER'S VIEW OF STAGE 1

The undeveloped group, team or organisation is a cold place where people are unable to express their feelings. Emotions are seen as appropriate only to private life and not to the workplace. Any show of feelings or emotions, should it occur, is seen as embarrassing and is either ignored or swept under the carpet. There is a degree of conformity, either because of inertia or because of fear to press changes, but there is certainly no restriction on whingeing. Even constructive ideas about change are unwelcome: the concept of not 'rocking the boat' is seen as very important and as a route to promotion. As a result of this passive acceptance, people often lack sparkle and the leadership, however misguided, is seldom assertively challenged. We are not ready for Role and Control issues to be settled.

Little care is shown for people or for what they have to say, in spite of the fact that people say a great deal. The school axiom 'God gave us two ears and one mouth for a purpose' is ignored: there is a lot of talking and little listening. Meetings consist of a series of statements attempting to define a position, but with no real relation to what has come before or is to follow. If errors are made or personal weaknesses appear, they are used as weapons against others or covered up. The group has no skill in learning from individual or group mistakes. The tacit assumption is that any Pairing and Sharing issues are not only premature but actually dangerous, in that groupings or pairs could well prejudice the Role and Control issues that are to come next.

There is no consensus on the purpose of the group or what needs to be done, and often the leader has a view that is completely different from that of those attempting to follow. Authority is accepted as a reason for acceptance, regardless of understanding or common sense. Outside threats are met with defensiveness, paperwork, reorganisations and new, more stifling, rules.

I discussed one organisation at the first stage with its boss. He explained that his subordinates had been making a number of errors lately, and that the main board were complaining. The

response had been to pass each document up the line with the
appropriate manager's signature:

'That way they will understand the concept of responsibility,
and we will know exactly who to blame when it goes wrong.'

Every team and organisation goes through the first phase of
development, and can be effective provided that the manager has
the time, wisdom and skills to make all the decisions. Stage 1 is not
an effective team but a number of individuals working for a boss.

Stage 2 – Role and Control: the developing team

What the individuals in the group are attempting:

To define the official and unofficial hierarchy within the group.
To establish roles.

The behaviours a fly on the wall will observe:

- Defensiveness, competition and jealousy.
- Challenges to the structure, nature and purpose of the task.
- Experimental hostility and aggressiveness.
- Ambivalence to the leader if appointed, and 'stag fights' for
  leadership if not.
- Testing of roles.
- 'Intense, brief and brittle links'.
- Clique and faction formation and decay.
- In tasks where high skill or commitment is needed from
  individuals – tantrums.

In tasks where there is an over-capacity of talents or labour –
prolonged searching for roles, and protectiveness.
Tensions, anxiety and rule-breaking.

It's a tough stage, but still one I call the developing team.

An outsider's view of Stage 2

The meeting of individual Role and Control needs begins when a
group decides to review its operating procedures. Something has
made it see that all the decisions cannot be made by the leader, and
that individuals are not developing – there has to be a better way.

The reader may remember Westbrown Holdings from Chapter 5. It
was a medium-size firm in Public Relations and Advertising run by

John West. John was a charismatic figure who chose to understand all the accounts and attend every presentation. He would say: 'When you think you are going to get an account, call me on the bleeper and arrange the meeting in an airport for twelve. There is nowhere in Europe you cannot get to by twelve . . .'

In the last chapter, I discussed the pressures on John. Now look at the way his behaviour held the team in Stage 1. Nobody was able to define his or her *own* role because everything had to be related back to John. This was a group of individuals working for a manager and it was quite obvious that this form of structure, as well as being individually stifling, was impossible as the firm grew. John himself realised the symptoms – low morale, high staff turnover, boring meetings, low creativity, lost opportunities, mutual blaming – all the Stage 1 issues. In practice, John called me in to conduct a weekend workshop for all his top managers, and together we lived through Stage 2 and, it is to be hoped, reached the point where we could see Stage 3 – but that comes later.

The Stage 2 organisation is testing: the members know they have actually joined and belonging is not an issue, but they just establish the Role and Control issues before individual relationships founded on respect and trust can be allowed to harden the structure of the team.

I began work with John's group by asking them to tell me what issues they considered part of the weekend's agenda. What came up were bland statements about 'improved communications' and 'better liaison with divisions', and more tentative questions about 'male and female issues'. On the Saturday one of the regional managers demanded that her problems be faced. She had been passed over for promotion in spite of having received excellent informal appraisals from John. The group agreed to face the issue and in the discussion, which lasted three hours, it faced real problems with true emotions. We recorded the issues that turned up and informal sub-committees dealt with them, returning to the plenary session in the evening. The organisation did appear to be male-dominated, although the members were largely female. There was a complete domination of decision-making by John, which was felt to be holding back many people in the regions and even at Head Office. Head Office was dominating control, and the problems of the regions were real.

Sunday was marked by one of the most apparently stable members of the staff breaking down completely, and being allowed by the group to explain how good work was largely ignored and all the effort was concentrated on the 'bad performer' – management's liberal attitude was counter-productive as far as she was concerned. John admitted that he was happy handling male anger, but was incapable of taking on female tears. Quite suddenly people began listening and understanding what was happening and the whole group set about reorganising itself, setting up new ground rules and procedures. A very definite set of job specifications or roles was agreed, a long way from those allowed by default at Stage 1 of the team. John accepted that he was loved and respected by the team, but that he himself had to adopt a more ritualistic role, as a partial figurehead. The fears that he expressed in taking up this role were discussed. A certain magic had happened in the group from which I, as the facilitator, was completely excluded. Some months later, I heard that the team was now working much more effectively and that they had, in my terminology, entered Stage 3. The regional manager who had precipitated the clash on the Saturday had found herself unable to agree with the new informal structures and had resigned.

Stage 2 for John's team consisted of coming together to review its operating procedures and of treating subjects previously taboo in an open manner. Wider options were considered, personal feelings were handled, and animosities were put on the table.

As in the case of John's team, at the end of the Stage 2 developing phase, everyone accepts finally that they have a place in the team and, after negotiation, understands and accepts their role or leaves. The battles that achieving these objectives brings are real and intense, but they are necessary to reach Stage 3 and consolidation. I have met cases where the outcome of a vigorous attempt to move through Stage 2 was failure. In one case, powerful individuals refused to accept any negotiation of role and restructuring, and the group resorted, for its own survival, to Stage 1, with total reliance on an unwilling leader.

Stage 3 – Pairing and Sharing: the consolidating team

Once the Role and Control issues of Stage 2 have been completed, the team can begin to develop working practices that are practical and personally acceptable. I often find that a team in Stage 3 demands new seating arrangements and decides on fairly tight procedures which are directed towards the most effective accomplishment of the task, and are not based on blind authority or precedent as they were in Stage 1. Because all the members of the team that remain have been involved in the formulation of the rules and procedures, their control is internal and does not involve the authority of management for enforcement. The Pairing and Sharing is real and based on affection, trust and respect. The team is able to share knowledge and there is no defensive posturing between sub-groups, factions, leaders and led.

John's team travelled directly into Stage 3 after the traumatic weekend, and found that a number of informal working parties were set up. One of the regional offices was closed, as was a section of Head Office: people who needed, and wanted to work together found themselves sharing rooms, or at least meeting in a regular way.

Stage 4: the mature team

The mature team acts pragmatically, or appropriately. Everyone in the team know his or her value and role. Everyone in the team knows the formal and informal mechanisms, and his or her chain of communication. Trust is not an issue, but flexibility is. We find messages on our benches such as:

'Jones came round but you were out. I found the correct papers and results, but thought you would not like to give him all the figures. What I quoted was . . .'

The mature team is a fine place to work, and I have worked in two or three in some thirty years. One was very successful, and one failed completely at a task that was probably impossible. I regard belonging to them as the high spots of my professional life.

The sad thing is that any change, and in particular changes of personnel, cause a team to regress to an earlier Stage. For instance, a mature team may well find that, with the introduction of new members, it has regressed to Role and Control issues; a Stage 3 team may be lost to Stage 1 through an apparently slight change of objectives. The manager needs to be very clear about the stages of a team's development. The requirements for rapidly setting up an effective team are simple:

1. Clear understandable objectives
2. Some form of informal get-together for introductions
3. A clear chain of responsibility and authority

4. Clear setting of roles and personal objectives
5. Local geography that is as undirected as possible

These probably sound very easy to meet, but unfortunately, as the veteran manager will tell you, are very rarely so in practice. Everything depends on having clear objectives, and in my experience most objectives resemble an archery target on a roller coaster. Try to get clear objectives, and to make certain of the other rules, because they are virtually under your control and they make life more effective.

The next chapter will take on the issue of role-setting, both for you as manager of a team and for a team member. I shall discuss management style and how to live in difficult mixes – with what I used to call awkward personalities, but now understand as personalities that react unfortunately with ourselves.

CHAPTER SEVEN

Teams, Team Roles and the Manager

Function and Task

'My style of management seems to be different – I like to organise people and my boss seems to want to push them all the time.'

'We have to work together but we seem to step on each other's toes all the time.'

'My problem is that I am always saying to people, "Go on, get out of my way, I'll do it".'

'I still like doing things.'

In the last chapter, I discussed the way that groups form into working teams through a series of well-defined steps, and I closed the discussion by giving a number of requirements for the speeding up of this process. In this chapter, I shall deal with one of these requirements: Clear roles for everyone. I shall discuss another one – Clear understandable objectives – in a later chapter.

A successful team needs to contain individuals with different characteristics performing different roles, and I shall give names to these roles. I shall quote a simple test from Belbin by which the reader can identify his or her own preferred role, or combination of roles, and see how this relates to management style. I shall discuss how the deliberate engineering of roles can make for a more effective team and can be related to the team's objective – established work, requiring different balances of individuals can contract with colleagues to avoid clashes. *I am discussing modifiable behaviour which can be highlighted by an inventory showing how you rate the functions of your job.*

As I have already said, any activity can be viewed from two different directions:

The Task – what is to be done
The Process – how it is being done

In some circumstances the Task has such overwhelming urgency
that the Process is swamped – the end totally submerges the
means; but, as I shall say again, in real terms and for lesser
purposes, *how* things are done matters a great deal. When the
lifeboats need to be manned and the ship is sinking fast, the person
able to take authority does what is necessary and individual
wishes are unimportant. Only when the lifeboat sights dry land
does the Process and our individuality regain importance.

Belbin studied the success rate of hundreds of managers working to solve management exercises in teams, and looked at many
variations in team composition. An early idea was that putting all
the most intelligent experts together would produce the most
successful teams – for example, experts in production, marketing,
finance – in fact the Apollo teams of the best people did not
produce anything like consistently good results. Belbin did try a
team composed of what were basically dull people and found that
they performed his exercises in a very mediocre way; but he also
found that by *planting* one exciting and creative person in the
group, the team's performance increased markedly. Finally, Belbin came up with the conclusion that, for a successful team,
certain specific process needs had to be respected, and that these
needs could be related to the psychometric tests he was able to run
on individuals. For instance, in a successful team somebody
should be concerned with the importance of general strategy and
see the need to translate it into practicable instructions: this
individual, he found, should be 'stable' and 'controlled'. It is also
necessary for someone to understand the importance of the detail
of completion, and this person will tend to be 'anxious' and
'introvert'. Anyone can pay lip-service to the process functions,
but Belbin finally came up with eight clusters of personality that
accepted the involvement, concern and genuine interest necessary
to fulfil the required roles over an extended period.

The Belbin Functions

Belbin identified eight Process functions that need to be *honoured*
in a successful team. It is virtually inconceivable that any team will
contain exactly eight people whose make-up fits respectively the
eight functions: teams of five are recommended, and of necessity

the functions will overlap. Not every team needs to contain each of the functions in the same measure: a team created for an innovatory role will have a different balance from one created for a holding role. What remains firm in Belbin's study of many teams is that, whatever the task a team is created to perform, each of the functions needs to be recognised, to be honoured in some way by a member of the team. Conversely, an over-capacity in particular functions leads to clashes and unproductive behaviour.

--------▶

EXERCISE
The Belbin Self-Perception Inventory

For each of the seven sections, distribute a total of ten points between the possible responses according to how you consider they best fit your own behaviour. The ten points can be distributed evenly, or perhaps all given to one single response. Enter the points at the side.

1. *What I believe I can contribute to a team:*

(a) I think I can quickly see and take advantage of new opportunities.
(b) I can work well with a wide range of people.
(c) Producing ideas is one of my natural assets.
(d) My ability rests in being able to draw people out when I detect something that can be contributed valuably to group activities.
(e) My capacity to follow through with projects has much to do with my personal effectiveness.
(f) I am ready to face temporary unpopularity if it leads to worthwhile results in the end.
(g) I can usually sense what is realistic and likely to work.
(h) I can offer a reasoned case for alternative courses of action without introducing bias or prejudice.

2. *If I have a shortcoming in team work, it could be:*

(a) I am not at ease unless meetings are well structured and generally well conducted.
(b) I am inclined to be generous towards others who have a valid viewpoint that has not been given a proper airing.
(c) I have a tendency to talk too much once the group gets on to new ideas.

(d) My objective outlook makes it difficult for me to join in with colleagues readily and enthusiastically.

(e) I am sometimes seen as forceful and authoritarian if there is a need to get something done.

(f) I find it difficult to lead from the front: perhaps I am over-responsive to group atmosphere.

(g) I am apt to get caught up in ideas that occur to me, and so lose track of what is happening.

(h) My colleagues tend to see me as worrying unnecessarily over detail and the possibility that things may go wrong.

3. *When involved in a project with other people:*

(a) I have an aptitude for influencing people without pressurising them.

(b) My general vigilance prevents careless mistakes and omissions being made.

(c) I am ready to press for action to make sure that the meeting does not waste time or lose sight of the main objectives.

(d) I can be counted on to contribute something original.

(e) I am always ready to back a good suggestion in the common interest.

(f) I am keen to look for the latest in new ideas and developments.

(g) I believe my capacity for judgement can help to bring about the right decisions.

(h) I can be relied upon to see that all essential work is organised.

4. *My characteristic approach to group work is that:*

(a) I have a quiet interest in getting to know colleagues better.

(b) I am not reluctant to challenge the views of others, or to hold a minority view myself.

(c) I can usually find a line of argument to refute unsound propositions.

(d) I think I have a talent for making things work once a plan has been put into operation.

(e) I have a tendency to avoid the obvious and come out with the unexpected.

(f) I bring a touch of perfection to any job I undertake.

(g) I am ready to make use of contacts outside the job itself.

(h) While I am interested in all views, I have no hesitation in making up my mind once a decision has to be made.

5. *I gain satisfaction in a job because:*

(a) I enjoy analysing situations and weighing up all the possible choices.
(b) I am interested in finding practical solutions to problems.
(c) I like to feel I am fostering good working relationships.
(d) I can have a strong influence on decisions.
(e) I can meet people who may have something new to offer.
(f) I can get people to agree on a necessary course of action.
(g) I feel in my element where I can give a task my full attention.
(h) I like to find a field that stretches my imagination.

6. *If I were suddenly given a difficult task with limited time and unfamiliar people:*

(a) I would feel like retiring to a corner to devise a way out of the impasse before developing a line.
(b) I would be ready to work with the person who showed the most positive approach.
(c) I would find some way of reducing the size of the task by establishing what different individuals might best contribute.
(d) My natural sense of urgency would help to ensure that we did not fall behind schedule.
(e) I believe I would keep cool and maintain my capacity to think straight.
(f) I would retain a steadiness of purpose in spite of the pressures.
(g) I would be prepared to take a positive lead if I felt the group was making no progress.
(h) I would open up discussions with a view to stimulating new thoughts and getting something moving.

7. *Thinking about the problems I have when working in groups, I can see that:*

(a) I am apt to show my impatience with those who are obstructing progress.
(b) Others may criticise me for being too analytical and insufficiently intuitive.
(c) My desire to ensure that work is properly done may hold up proceedings.

(d) I tend to get bored rather easily and rely on one or two stimulating members to spark me off.

(e) I find difficulty starting unless the goals are clear.

(f) I am sometimes poor at explaining and clarifying complex points that occur to me.

(g) I am conscious of wanting from others what I cannot do myself.

(h) I hesitate to get my points across against real opposition.

Make sure that the points in each set add up to ten and the total for all seven sets is 70.

Before I ask you to analyse the results of your Self-Perception Inventory, I would like you to see whether you are likely to agree with its findings. Belbin gave names to each of the personality clusters he found related to the necessary functions required for the processes of an effective team.

Read through the brief descriptions opposite and mark them High, Medium or Low according to your view of yourself as a team member.

In a successful team all eight roles need to be honoured, to a greater or lesser degree, depending on the task.

Complete the following form and add up the totals in order to produce your Belbin profile. Note that the analysis table 'decodes' the scores, and is not a simple addition of the scores. For instance, if your score in Section 1 was a=1, b=4, c=2, d=0, e=1, f=2, g=0 and h=0, then using the decoding table your first row would be:

Section	CW		CH		SH		PL		RI		ME		TW		CF	
1	g	0	d	0	f	2	c	2	a	1	h	0	b	4	e	1

Now let's add up your scores:

Section	CW	CH	SH	PL	RI	ME	TW	CF
1	g	d	f	c	a	h	b	e
2	a	b	e	g	c	d	f	h
3	h	a	c	d	f	g	e	b
4	d	h	b	e	g	c	a	f
5	b	f	d	h	e	a	c	g
6	f	c	g	a	h	e	b	d
7	e	g	a	f	d	b	h	c
TOTAL								

Role name	Role definition
Company Worker (CW)	Converter of concepts, strategy and ideas into relevant plans for action.
Chairman (CH)	Charismatic steerer from non-productive strife towards focusing resources.
Shaper (SH)	Forceful person who has the task in mind and makes sure everyone else does it.
Plant (PL)	The ideas person who finds new angles and approaches to problems.
Resource Investigator (RE)	The Mr/Mrs Fix-it who has contacts and runs the relevant and irrelevant networks.
Monitor Evaluator (ME)	The standard setter who knows how it was and how it should be done.
Team Worker (TW)	The person wanting to get on with the job without the hassle of control issues.
Completer Finisher (CF)	The actual completer of jobs and the one concerned with fine details.

In the notes that follow, I am going to detail the likely behaviours of individuals whose *predominant* functioning lies in one of Belbin's eight categories. In my experience of analysing the characteristics of many individuals, the total predominance of one category is very rare indeed. Most of us behave in accordance with several of Belbin's categories, the intensity of our personal involvement varying throughout the eight. When we read the discrete personality profiles we need to internalise by joining several profiles together, accepting that our own personality may on balance contain measures of each exclusive profile, from a high measure to perhaps an insignificant one. The low as well as the high preferences are important when we consider our preferred team behaviour. When, for any reason we wish to change our behaviour in a particular team, we need to understand our complete profile.

THE COMPANY WORKER

The Company Worker possesses a psychometric profile of being stable and controlled and is perceived by others as a practical organiser. The Company Worker is able to take general instructions and convert these into defined and manageable tasks. A Company Worker makes workable plans out of rough concepts by the application of logic.

The Company Worker has strength of character and is able to apply a disciplined approach to most things. The characteristics of loyalty, sincerity, integrity and controlled personal ambition allow him or her to inspire the trust necessary to perform the function. The Company Worker can be flummoxed by sudden changes of plan or by too much uncertainty. He or she is attempting to bring order out of chaos, but the function is possible only if the chaos is containable.

The Company Worker needs stable structures and is not happy unless the Role and Control issues are settled. If they are not, then their resolution is the first priority. Once these are resolved, the new priority will be the conversion of decisions into schedules, and workers into organisational structures. The work is systematic, methodical and efficient, but at times too unresponsive to the speculative and what is characterised as 'airy-fairy', which is not seen as having any direct visible or immediate bearing on the fascinating organisational problems in hand – we are *How* people and not *Why* people. There is, however, a willingness to trim and adapt schedules and proposals to plans and proposals coming by agreement or through the hierarchy. The Company Worker is conscious of status.

The consciousness of status, particularly status within the team, can produce unconstructive criticism of other, 'lower', members of the team.

Above all, the Company Worker is perceived as the *controller* of knowledge within the team. He or she is the person who functions through knowledge and whose expertise is drawn on first by members of the team who want up-to-date information.

THE CHAIRMAN

The Chairman (I prefer this word to the de-sexed but more clumsy 'Chairperson') comes out as a stable, dominant extrovert on Belbin's psychometric tests. He or she may not be the hierarchical leader of the team, but will certainly be able to carry out a leadership role if required. The Chairman in the Belbin team functions as the co-ordinator of people and things in the team's efforts to meet external goals and targets. This co-ordinating function is done through personality or charisma and not by deploying more readily identifiable skills.

The Chairman is normally intelligent without being brilliant, recognises ideas without being a prime originator, and finds him- or herself 'chosen' without having had to push for influence. The Chairman is disciplined and has 'natural' authority: he or she is dominant without being domineering. There is a sensibly controlled natural instinct to trust, which inspires trust and confidence in others. There is also a lack of competitiveness which undercuts jealousy.

The ability to focus others on their strengths and the ability to get others to work effectively together often mean that the Chairman establishes the roles and the work boundaries of the other team members, and works towards a balance of functions by adjustment, pruning and importation.

The Chairman communicates well and appropriately – to peers, superiors and subordinates.

The Chairman is concerned vitally with the team's objectives and, seeing it as important that they remain clear, spends much time in both clarification and agenda-setting. He or she sets priorities, but is less concerned with the nitty-gritty of the work. Early contributions are likely to be in the form of questions, accurate listening and paraphrasing, feedback and summarising. If a decision is appropriate, he or she will take the clear Chairman's prerogative of the 'casting vote'.

An effective Chairman is sought after both in formal work situations and in leisure-based activities. The Chairman in the office may well also be the Chairman of the Dahlia Club.

THE SHAPER

Psychometric tests link the Shaper with the anxious, dominant extrovert. We may suppose that teams need different types of leadership. The Company Worker may structure and delegate, while the Chairman provides social leadership. The task leader is the Shaper who is in charge of a specific project and makes sure it is done.

The Shaper is full of nervous energy, outgoing, emotional, impulsive, impatient, sometimes edgy, and easily frustrated. The Shaper is quick to challenge and quick to respond to challenge –

challenge is actually welcomed. The Shaper often finds him- or herself in dispute, and has rows which have a spontaneous quality – quick to rise and quick to vanish without trace, a phenomenon which often confuses others. Of all the team members, the extreme Shaper is most prone to the paranoia of sensing and personalising slights and conspiracies. The Shaper wants it his or her way, and has an animal nose for scenting challenge. The Shaper has a high Control need, and very often a Critical Parent-dominated personality.

The principal function of a Shaper in a team is to focus and mould the team's efforts, using a much more direct input than the Chairman. He or she is looking for patterns in discussions, and tries to unite ideas and objectives so that simple and practicable actions can be decided upon and pushed into practice as soon as possible.

Shapers exude self-confidence, which often conceals strong self-doubts. Confidence comes through actual measurable results. The drive, which may well have a compulsive quality, is directed to the team's objectives as defined by the Shaper. The coincidence of team and Shaper objectives may be real, but there is always a suspicion that the Shaper sees the team as a tool, an extension of his or her own ego. The permanent wish is for action, and action now.

The competitive nature and the intolerance of delays or wooliness, of any form of weakness or vagueness or muddled thinking, are inclined to make others attribute arrogance to the Shaper. People within the team may often abhor the Shaper's timing, and regard him or her as a steamroller. At best, however, the Shaper is the individual in the team who makes things happen, even if they have to happen the Shaper's own way. At worst, the Shaper *is* a steamroller. Conflicts between more than one Shaper in a team can, of course, be less than productive.

THE PLANT

The Plant is the first of the team roles as I am listing them to be associated with IQ – Plants are bright, introverted and tend towards the dominant.

The name 'Plant' originates from a management practice of 'planting' a controversial and creative member into uninspired or ineffective teams with a view to increasing performance. The Plant, at his or her most effective is able to scatter seeds of inspiration for others to cultivate and bring to fruition. No seeds – no crop.

The Plant is the team's source of original ideas, suggestions and proposals. Other team members will, of course, have ideas, but what distinguishes the Plant's ideas is their originality and the radical-minded approach. The Plant has a detached way of seeing from the outside, unhampered by the here-and-now reality: he or she has no problems with the concept of the Management Helicopter – the problem is landing it. The Plant is likely to have a strong Natural Child, forever asking Why? and perhaps more significantly Why not?, and could be the most imaginative as well as the most intelligent member of the team. The Plant is most likely to start searching for new angles when the team begins to get bogged down. He or she is also likely to bring new ideas to a problem even after a course of action has been settled, and to miss out details and make careless mistakes with unrepentant abandon.

The Plant is thrustful and uninhibited in a way that is uncharacteristic of the introvert. His or her people needs may be at either extreme. The Plant can be prickly and cause offence to other members of the team, particularly when dealing with other people's ideas. Criticisms of a Plant are likely to result in counter-proposals.

The danger of the Plant's efforts in a team is that too much competitive energy will be devoted to exciting new ideas, regardless of whether they fall in with the team's needs or contribute to its objectives. Timing is not a Plant skill. The Plant is likely to be bad at taking criticism of his or her own ideas, and quick to take offence and sulk if the ideas are not immediately accepted with appropriate praise. If the Plant's ideas are not welcomed, he or she may well refuse to contribute further. Working effectively with Plants takes a great deal of skill, and the other team members (usually the Chairman) need to use skills approaching and including flattery to get the most from them.

Whatever their faults, *Plants provide the vital spark*.

RESOURCE INVESTIGATOR

The Resource Investigator shows as a stable, dominant extrovert and is probably the most obviously likeable in the whole team. He or she is relaxed, sociable and gregarious, with a ready and easily aroused interest giving positive and enthusiastic responses to new ideas. However, his or her stamina with ideas, things and people is low – matters that are quickly taken up are as quickly put down. He or she may have high Joining and Belonging and Role needs and probably works from Little Professor.

The Resource Investigator moves outside the group and brings information and ideas back. He or she is the Mr or Ms Fix-it who runs networks of contacts, always 'knowing somebody who . . .' He or she is mobile, seldom in the office to be contacted on routine matters, and when in the office is probably running up phone bills. The Resource Investigator is the perpetual salesperson, the liaison officer, the public relations person, exploring new ideas and possibilities from the world outside and returning to the team like a cat with a mouse it has caught – expecting praise, whatever the mouse's condition. The Resource Investigator's ability to stimulate new ideas and to encourage innovation can lead people to mistake him or her for an ideas person, but there is no radical originality. This is a communicator, a collector and an adapter.

Without the stimulus of others or of change, the Resource Investigator can easily become bored, demoralised and ineffective. Solitary jobs are not on the menu. Within the team, he or she can be a good improviser, active under pressure, and a driving force who is unfortunately inclined to over-relax when things ease. A principal failing is that of not following up tasks begun in enthusiasm – the bursts of energy can well be short-lived. The range and variety of outside interests may well lead him or her into irrelevances, and the team may feel a lack of any true loyalty. The Mr or Ms Fix-it is very much his or her own person, whose efforts as a contact person or gate-keeper may be valued more by outsiders than by the team itself. When Resource Investigators are ready, they leave.

The Resource Investigator's role is to preserve the team from stagnation and to give it a view of the outside world that may increase both its effectiveness and its chance of survival in a political world.

MONITOR EVALUATOR

The Monitor Evaluator is, like the Plant, a possessor of a high IQ and an introvert. He or she is stable without the paranoia or the quest for dominance. The Monitor Evaluator, unlike the moody live-wire Plant, comes across as a bit of a cold fish – someone to be watched, perhaps because he or she seems to be watching you. By temperament the Monitor Evaluator is likely to be serious, and the contribution lies in measurement and dispassionate analysis rather than creativity. Unlikely to produce an original proposal, the function is likely to prevent the team from committing itself to foolish acts. He or she is likely to have well-developed Critical Parent and Adult, and to have a low overall need for human contact, but to be always striving for a clear role.

By nature a critic rather than an originator, the Monitor Evaluator does not make criticism for its own sake, but often almost compulsively when a flaw is seen. This may cause friction with the Plant because, in one very important way, they are similar: both see things in the abstract and not in the concrete – the Plant seeking the new, and the Monitor Evaluator the precedent. Neither is pragmatic.

Least motivated to action of all the team members, euphoria and enthusiasm for action are foreign to the character. The compensating factor is that personal involvement does not cloud or distort the Monitor Evaluator's judgement: he or she is slow to make up the mind, wanting time to mull things over, but objective to the point of awkwardness.

One of this functionary's skills lies in assimilating, relating and evaluating volumes of complex material, and in assessing the views and judgements of others. Since this is done in the abstract, the results can often be presented at the 'wrong time' or tactlessly. This lack of political and social skills can often lower the team's morale and, of course, make the Monitor Evaluator less than popular. It can also lower credibility, particularly when the team is under stress and the Shaper and Chairman are calling for concerted action. The criticisms coming from the Monitor Evaluator may be seen, quite unfairly, as a challenge for power by the Chairman or Shaper. The Monitor Evaluator is concerned with the task and is personally unambitious, so such a response to his or her 'help' is unexpected.

Monitor Evaluators need to learn to be responsive to change, or they become depressingly negative and defensive about the past and its failures. Solid and dependable but often perceived as joyless and cold, they need to be listened to and their judgement welcomed by a successful team.

TEAM WORKER

The Team Worker is the most sensitive member of the team, being aware of and reacting to the emotional undercurrents, and being concerned with the private lives and concerns of the others. The Team Worker is a stable, non-dominant extrovert who is an active but quiet communicator, popular and unassertive. He or she is loyal to the team as a unit, and, although able to take sides should the need arise, prefers the support role while getting on with the job. The Team Worker is a 'grafter' who very often has a special expertise, and who likes to build on others' ideas without feeling the necessity to produce counter-concepts. I would see the Team

Worker as having high needs for Joining and Belonging and Pairing and Sharing, but low Control needs, working from Nurturing Parent.

A good and willing listener who is able to communicate freely and well within the team, the Team Worker encourages others to do the same. He or she likes harmony and accord, and is willing to work hard to promote it in others. Often the Team Worker is able to counterbalance the frictions caused by the Shaper and Plant, and on occasion by the Monitor Evaluator, but he or she has limits. The Team Worker dislikes personal confrontation and may well leave an unhappy team for this reason. Unlike the Chairman, for him or her the resolution of conflict is about an inner concern that conflict is bad in itself, even if the conflict in fact serves a necessary purpose in the development of the task.

When the team is under pressure or in difficulties, the Team Worker's sympathy, understanding, loyalty and support are invaluable. His or her uncompetitiveness and dislike of personal confrontation may appear as indecisiveness or even as weaknesses, but these qualities also make for a permanent force operating against division and disruption in the team. The Team Worker's role paradoxically is most felt in absence, especially in times of stress and pressure. The Team Worker is, in Hertzberg's terms, a hygiene factor – noticed most by its absence. As he or she is also the 'grafter' who likes to get on with the job, and with other people without concern for politics, the Team Worker needs to receive conscious nourishment from the more 'noisy' members of the team.

If a team takes too long in the Role and Control battles the Team Worker leaves – at the very time when perhaps most needed.

COMPLETER FINISHER

The Completer Finisher is an anxious introvert who likes to see things done properly. He or she is the 'dotter of i's and the crosser of t's', the checker, the 'wait a minute – that can't go out like that' person who can drive the Plant and the Shaper to distraction. The very mention of the words 'Hurry up' will produce conflict.

The extreme Completer Finisher expresses his or her anxiety through obsessive behaviour, continually checking and re-checking, regardless of the external pressures and the pragmatic reasons for closure. Such behaviour on a lesser scale may still be perceived as annoying fussiness.

The Completer Finisher is not an assertive member of the team, but maintains a permanent sense of urgency which communicates itself to others and can well galvanise them to action. The

Completer Finisher has a personal discipline and strength of character which resists outside pressures, hating the casual or slapdash. He or she carries the conscience of the team for missed schedules, betrayed customers or over-promises. I would expect the Completer Finisher to have low Joining and Belonging needs and probably quite strong Pairing and Sharing needs. The Critical Parent is likely to dominate and, under extreme provocation, take over.

The major preoccupation of the Completer Finisher is with order: order has an importance beyond pragmatism, and he or she is the compulsive perfectionist. This compulsion to 'getting it right' obviously brings the individual into stress, and will certainly bring the individual into conflict with the other team members.

A controlled Completer Finisher is an essential member, the need for whom can easily be overlooked. In many teams, the Completer Finisher is so much lacking in 'honour' as to be relegated to 'another floor'. This lack of 'honour' for the role has a serious effect on the team's performance and leads to unnecessary vulnerability. Badly managed, the Completer Finisher can be allowed to be a moaner, bogged down in small and irrelevant details. He or she is a challenge to effective management and, as a real part of the team, can make the major contribution to the setting of objectives and standards. The relentless follow-through is a team asset to be valued.

———▶

EXERCISE

Look at the profiles of Ian and Kathy overleaf.

How would their management styles differ?

What jobs would most suit them *in their present state of development*?

———————▶

The Belbin role profiles, at their best, indicate the way in which we have adapted to our jobs and, if we are to be successful, how we need to adapt our teams and jobs to ourselves. They indicate behaviour profiles and, as such, they are subject to change and adaptation. We have found that individuals in very staid jobs are inclined to have very pronounced patterns, whereas people embarking on their careers are inclined to have a more neutral pattern, with each role being honoured.

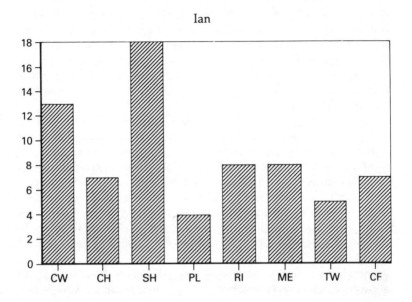

Ian

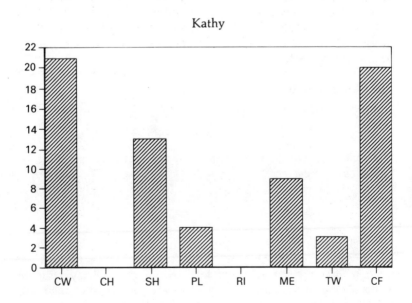

Kathy

Let's look at Ian first. Ian's energies lie in Shaper (SH) and
Company Worker (CW). He does recognise the other functions,
but his real interests lie in sorting out instructions (CW) and in
actually getting others to follow them (SH). I can see Ian doing
well in his chosen profession, that of production manager. He
recognises the need for the professional charm of the Chairman,
for the skills networking from the Resource Investigator, for the
monitoring of how things are done by the Monitor Evaluator, and
for the Completer Finisher's function of making sure that they are
done correctly in all their detail. His lowest categories are Team
Worker, whose functions are to do with actually 'working' and
having warm feelings towards one's fellow workers, and Plant,
whose function is the provision of new ideas.

Kathy is strong on Company Worker and Completer Finisher.
She will be able to convert strategy to tactics, and will have
considerable concern about the detailed viability of what results
from her work. She is also strong on Shaper and is concerned with
moving things along. She was the senior manager in charge of a
contracts department of a firm specialising in exports. Legally
vague and technically skilled salespersons would sell products in
large volumes to literally hundreds of countries. Her job was to
make sure that the company made money out of the orders.

Look at your own pattern and consider whether it matches the
job you have to fulfil. The profile is not perfect, so look back at the
questions, for these are the fundamental ones about how you see
the working world.

Before we go on to the last point of this chapter, have a look at
the profile of Bob:

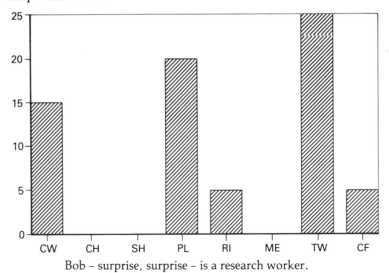

Bob – surprise, surprise – is a research worker.

The team

Teams are made up of individuals who, if we are to be successful, complete the jigsaw of roles in a way that is appropriate to the job the team is called upon to accomplish. A production group, for example, needs all the functions, but perhaps the Plant and the Chairman might be less important than the Shaper. Too many Shapers, however, will conflict with each other, and perhaps one strong Shaper in charge would be best. If that Shaper were poor in the Company Worker function, or accepted that he must delegate it, then the team would function more effectively.

I have done a considerable amount of work with supermarket managers. In looking at many managers, I reached two successful profiles – the first being dominated by Shaper, the second by Company Worker. Stores run by the Shapers have a high staff turnover and I have the vision of everything being controlled and held by a single firm manager. He or she has a high profile in the store. The Company Worker-managed store has regular meetings of department managers, who have clear instructions and accept their responsibilities. His or her managers stay, and are seen on the store floor. They have the visibility, and come to rely on their manager for support when things go wrong. If things go horribly wrong, their manager can panic, whereas the Shaper-controlled staff know that the manager will cope magnificently.

Management style needs to adapt to the team, and of course the team needs to adapt to the management style. Look at this team:

Role	CW	CH	SH	PL	RI	ME	TW	CF
MD	15	8	11	7	3	12	9	5
Production Manager	6	11	10	14	7	8	6	8
Marketing Manager	8	22	10	2	2	7	12	7
Finance Manager	8	10	11	9	8	12	5	7
Team Totals	37	51	42	32	20	39	22	27

The team as a whole is probably weak in political contacts since Resource Investigator is its lowest point. It is also a team of managers: someone else will have to deal with the Team Worker functions, and they had better have a second level of management to make up the deficiency. Otherwise the team is balanced and should be successful.

How should the manager attempt to manage such a team?

	CW	CH	SH	PL	RI	ME	TW	CF
MD	15	8	11	7	3	12	9	5

I would suggest that the style be consultative, using all the skills of the group, and looking towards controlling *how* things are done by means of the Monitor Evaluator function. The manager should use his (in this case) Company Worker skills to provide clearly defined and agreed work patterns for his colleagues.

Another and different team was:

Role	CW	CH	SH	PL	RI	ME	TW	CF
MD	12	22	10	16	1	0	10	0
Production	20	8	6	7	10	11	4	4
Marketing	11	10	18	2	7	11	7	4
Finance	5	2	13	10	4	22	5	9
Totals	48	42	47	35	22	44	26	17

I would expect the MD to have to use an inspirational/charismatic style. He will be a creative manager whose traps will be to get 'rabbit-holed' into ideas (high Plant score) and personally involved (high Team Worker score). Challenges are likely from Finance through the Monitor Evaluator function ('That's not the way!') and from Marketing through the Shaper function ('Go on – *tell* them'). The Company Worker in Production may also despise the lack of clarity of the instructions. In practice, the team did break down and split into in- and out-groups.

Look at your own patterns and those of your team. Teams fail when:

Roles are over-represented.
Roles are absent.
The balance of totals does not fit the task.
The management style is unsuitable for the team composition or the task.

In the next chapter, I shall extend the discussion of the management role, and attempt to answer the question: 'Yes but what do I actually do?'

CHAPTER EIGHT

The Role of the Manager

Yes, but what do I actually do?

'I'm told to set objectives . . . how?'

'I see myself as a sort of facilitator, but my boss doesn't see it that way at all.'

'Communicating with other departments is the difficulty; they seem to have a different set of values.'

'When I was a worker I knew the score. Now I seem to be judged on the basis of not being noticed – it's hard.'

'Management is the direction of resources, including people, towards a goal.' The definition seems simple enough, but what we have already seen on our journey may have already given us qualms. Nearly every word of the definition can be extended and discussed. Each word brings more questions to mind, and could be extended like a President Kennedy speech:

'Management, and by management I mean the facilitating, the control, the influencing and if necessary the inspiring, of resources – resources may be the renewable, vital gifts of the earth, and management then may be a noble struggle against nature . . .'

The definition *could* be extended in that way, but perhaps not usefully.

I have already discussed the issues that make an art out of the direction of others, and shown how there are individual issues and group issues. I have also indicated that we ourselves are likely to have preferred ways of carrying out our 'direction'. Some of us, for instance, push people into doing things, and others prefer cold organisational guidance. All the time, I have used the word 'goal'. Management is not doing things for our health or that of our subordinates. It is working for a purpose, and if we do not understand the purpose properly, then we cannot manage effectively. This chapter will begin by the analysis of goals.

'If you don't know where you're going, then you'll finish up somewhere else'

A manager has to understand, to an appropriate level, the task his or her team is to perform. Perhaps the most common complaint I hear from managers is concerned with this single issue. We very often receive woolly orders and – less excusably – *give* woolly orders. At a recent conference on the management of technology, the managing director of a major company described his instructions when he took up his first appointment to the board. The Chairman said:

> 'Just get things going. It's a virtually impossible job; nobody else has got within a mile. I want you to do your best, and don't forget – my ear is always available if you need to know anything.'

And that was that . . . He was left to 'get things going'. The experience of this conference key speaker is by no means unusual, and certainly matches my own experience:

> 'Look, just get on with it and do your best – do you want me to do your job for you?'

Such have been the retreating words of thousands of managers.
In giving instructions, *begin with clear objectives*:

DEFINE OBJECTIVES
AGREE STANDARDS
SET TARGETS

The objectives are where your and your team's efforts contribute to the organisation. The standards are a set of yardsticks against which all your staff can be judged. The targets are individually negotiated pointers designed to stretch and assess effort and capability.

————————➤

EXERCISE

Think of one task and the individual or team you have to direct to perform that task.

1. What is the overall objective of the task?
   Why does it need to be done?
   What in principle needs to be done?
   How do you feel it could be done and what are the likely consequences?

2. What standards do you wish to impose?
   Who needs to be satisfied?
   What time limit is there and how much money can be spent, or alternatively, how much money needs to be made?
   What resources of people or equipment are available?
   What external factors need to be considered (customer complaints, noise, publicity . . .)?
   What legal or organisational constraints are there ('the company would never let us do it that way')?

3. In the light of the constraints, review your objectives and convert these objectives into clear standards for all the team. Standards are those things that they *must* conform to.

4. Consider how you would communicate both the objectives and standards to your team. Remember you are now in a position to be *directive* and to give Critical Parent to Adult instructions.

5. Consider individuals in your team and look at the targets you could set. The standards are the *must* objectives, whereas the targets are the *improved* objectives. Think of them in terms of a non-swimmer being asked to jump across a river. It is essential – a *must* objective – that he or she jumps across the really deep bit, in order to avoid drowning, but a real bonus – an *improved* objective – would be gained if the non-swimmer managed to cross without getting wet at all.

————————➤

The method that I have begun to discuss in the example is based on the very detailed processes of Kepner and Tregoe, who sprang to fame in connection with the logical way in which NASA was able to correct faults in various rocket and lander systems. The Kepner

– Tregoe system, which was for me the first breakthrough in a rational understanding of the management job, tackles the setting of objectives in a number of distinct stages. (Kepner and Tregoe, who wrote in the 1970s, may not entirely recognise some of the features I have found it useful to evolve from their system.)

Let's take an example. Suppose we are asked to solve a problem of packages falling off pallets in a factory. The conversation at the Monday morning meeting might go something like this:

'I blame the new shift foreman – hasn't got the control.'

'I think that if we got that shrink-wrapping machine working properly, then there would be no problem.'

'At present we are losing about ten minutes every hour of the warehouseman's time.'

'Could we go back to the old band system?'

'No, that would give us problems with the end-users . . .'

The confusion between *Why, What, How* and *If* questions could go on for ever, but quite suddenly the Chairman says, looking directly at us:

'Seems like your sort of problem – set your team on it. Now, do we have any other business?'

Nobody in their right mind would suggest that each and every time one has a new task it is necessary to go laboriously through the stages I shall discuss – nothing would ever get done. What I am saying is that having the structure in your mind will help with almost every new task, and that certain tasks cry out for such an Adult, logical approach. I shall now try to work through the example, using this approach.

STRUCTURED PROBLEM ANALYSIS
STAGE 1: INITIAL CONCEPTION OF THE PROBLEM

The company is losing money because things are falling off pallets. The task the Chairman has given us is to reduce the number of things falling off and our problem is to find out how to do this. We have a clear *Why, What, How* and *If* statement of the problem, but *that is no possible use to our subordinates:* they need to know a lot more, and therefore we have to find out a lot more.

STAGE 2: DEFINING CONSTRAINTS

You can look at five categories of constraint upon any task – the constraints are as a cage imposed upon your and your team's work by the outside world of seniors, organisations and the environment in general.

1. *The customer.* Somebody has to be satisfied when the job is completed. In my simple example of the self-emptying pallets in the factory, the person who has to be satisified, the customer, is certainly the works manager, and we already know he likes things done just so . . . As a New Manager it is very important that you always find out who your customer is. Be assertive if your boss delegates responsibility downward: 'Write me a paper for the Governors' is an instruction that puts us on a collision course. All we could ever do is to write a paper to brief the people who control us, for them to develop as required. Work always has a political angle, and the wise New Manager lets others fight their own battles: 'When elephants fight the grass gets crushed' is a Hindu proverb that contains sound advice for any New Manager.

2. *Time and money.* Any task that does not involve the violation of the Second Law of Thermodynamics can, in my view, be cracked, given sufficient time and money. Monkeys, given virtually infinite time, will be able to write at least parts of certain Shakespearian plays. The problem is that even the universe with all its resources is unlikely to be able to give them that much time and energy. So it is with the tasks we are asked to do as managers. We need to get the job in perspective, in terms of the time and resources it is worth. In our pallet task we might find that a solution is needed in the next few weeks, and certainly before the summer shutdown. It also has to cost less than ten minutes an hour of a warehouseman's time. Wild and extended solutions are therefore not required. We also know that the boss is able to call for capital expenditure of up to £500 without endorsement by the board.

3. *The human resources.* The people working in a factory, our own team, our managers, all have limitations in terms of knowledge, skills and aptitudes. If the organisation will allow us to import specialists for a particular task, we need to know. Otherwise, we shall have to operate with our own human resources and all their limitations. For instance, if the factory is relatively low in technology, then high technology solutions will be inappropriate. The availability of human resources is a real constraint.

4. *The environment.* Any task has to be performed in accordance with a realistic estimate of the surrounding factors. If labour

relations are already difficult in the factory, a proposal for a procedure involving some discretion on the part of the workforce could be unwise. The factory may be very busy at present, but the planned shutdown happens in a few weeks. If there is already an environmental problem over waste disposal, increasing waste is inadvisable.

5. *Legal and organisational issues.* Patents, licences, legal constraints, conditions of work, custom and practice, company image . . . all these affect your way of doing a task and, as a New Manager, you need to understand them. 'If you do anything wrong, I'll let you know' is an attitude that presents great problems to the New Manager. Being able to check things out with a peer is a considerable advantage.

STAGE 3: REDEFINING THE TASK

Looking at the objectives of the task in a structured way allows us to redefine the instructions *as we see them.* I suggest that, in an area that matters, you prepare a problem definition of up to 200 words and share it with your manager:

> 'I see that you want recommendations for a quick and simple solution to the problem of packages falling off pallets. It is to involve capital expenditure of not more than £500, to use existing staff working not more than two hours a week overtime, and to be implemented during the factory shutdown period in August.'

The redefinition may be a little cheeky in that you will certainly have to guess some of the constraints; and your boss will certainly need to check some of the information; but for a few moments in your life as a manager, you and your boss will agree exactly on what you are doing, and this must be good.

STAGE 4: SETTING STANDARDS

Your staff are now in a position to hear what you want from them: 'The objective of the exercise is . . .' – and you tell them. Possible solutions to be investigated *must*:

1. Cost less than £500 in capital outlay.

2. Be fully detailed and ready for implementation during the summer shutdown.

3. Use existing staff and not interfere with other operational and development programmes.

4. Not violate any existing work practices or agreements.

5. Not involve more than two hours per week overtime for the immediate operators.

The targets that you lay down could be:

1. Capital expenditure of less than £500, and aim for the use of existing parts.

2. Running cost as near nil as possible, and aim for a solution that actually increases the speed of loading.

3. A clever idea that does not involve any shutdown time whatever.

The really bright workers in your team can go for the targets, but you will have to accept that they have been doing their jobs if they only meet the conditions you laid down.

If we can understand the task, then we can proceed to seeing what the job of a manager actually entails.

The manager's job

A manager works with groups and individuals towards a goal within the constraints of the organisation and the real world. The job involves continually balancing the needs of the task against the needs of individuals and of the whole team. It is necessary to understand and accept the fact that the team is at a particular point of development, and to act accordingly. An undeveloped team, with its requirement for Joining and Belonging, will wish its Role and Control needs to be held by the manager. The skilled manager recognises when to back off.

———▶

EXERCISE

Take two sheets of paper.
Head the first sheet: *Functions I need from good team members.*
Head the second sheet: *Things I hope to provide as a good team leader.*
Now fill in the two sheets, thinking of the things related to the *task* and to the *process*, with the aim of maintaining both individual and team performance.
When you have completed both the sheets, compare them. You

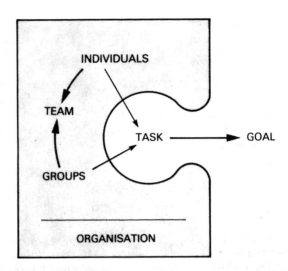

may well find that the team role analysis you completed in Chapter 7 fits what you now have in front of you. Your strengths and weaknesses in the Belbin roles should be reflected in what you require, need, do not require, and do not need in your team.

A team exists to fulfil a purpose, and when that purpose is strong enough, the individual needs of the team members are swamped by the actions in pursuit of that purpose. In real teams and for lesser purposes, the individual needs for Joining and Belonging, for Role and Control, for Pairing and Sharing, surface and can easily sabotage the effectiveness of the team. It is the duty of the team members to reduce the chances of such sabotage by dealing with individual needs, and of the leader to facilitate such activity. The team has needs itself as it passes through the stages of development, and it is both a collective and an individual responsibility that the team grow appropriately towards its goal. The division between management effort and individual team member effort in maintaining the personal and the team needs depends on the management style of the leader and on the team roles of the members.

In each category of behaviour, for both leader and team member, there is a positive and a negative set of aspects. What constitute positive behaviours and what constitute negative behaviours in working teams? In the first list we will look at the *task*-centred behaviours. The positive behaviours are concerned with enabling the work of the group to progress without the involvement of individuals except as means to that end. The negative behaviours are all concerned with attention-seeking and are signs that the individual needs of the group members are not being met. The manager with low human contact needs may well find him- or herself faced with more of such behaviours than is useful.

WORKING TOWARDS THE TASK

Positive	*Negative*
Information-giving, presentation of data in an effective manner	Production of red herrings, suppression of good data, poor information supply
Questioning or opinion-seeking inside or outside the group	Dismissing, blocking
Seeking clarification, reaching personal understanding, forcing clear thinking	Confusing, over-talking
Structuring, providing techniques or expertise to collate data	Dominating, premature foreclosure, clowning
Expediting, driving the task towards completion within time and other constraints	Withdrawal detachment
Quality control, assistance in making decisions and judgements in the work of the group	False hurry-up, personal spitefulness, aggression
Expertise, plain work	Virtually any egocentric behaviour

MAINTAINING THE TEAM

Positive	*Negative*
Providing for material needs, Making sure that the group and its members are free from distractions and interruptions	Any other business

and concerns from outside the
workplace
Provision of equipment and
services

Listening and observing and acting appropriately	Acting inappropriately, withdrawal
Team role adaptation to meet needs and reduce tension	Competitive behaviour
Setting and conforming to standards	Display behaviour
Honouring the stages of the group and helping it to progress	Regression of group's growth stages

MEETING INDIVIDUAL NEEDS

Positive	*Negative*
Expressing feelings and needs authentically, appropriately and assertively	Allowing personal issues to fester in self or others
Personal concern for the needs of others	Aggressive or passive behaviour where inappropriate
Sharing and empathic expression	Mocking behaviour

The lists are by no means complete, but as I write I can see a
pattern emerging. The word 'appropriate' comes to mind again
and again as the key to good team behaviour.

─────────▶

EXERCISE

Choose a meeting where you are able to act as an observer
without endangering your job.

Record which members of the team make positive contributions to effectiveness, and how often. Classify the contributions
as follows:

Task functions
1. Initiates and makes suggestions
2. Clarifies points

3. Summarises and is aware of time constraints
4. Asks for information and questions
5. Makes sure that decisions are clear and understood

Group maintenance
1. Checks out understanding
2. Brings in contributions
3. Encourages appropriately exhaustive exploration of ideas
4. Suggests ground rules and guidelines
5. Confronts where necessary
6. Appears to be sensitive to the stage of the group's development
7. Supports where necessary
8. Is able to provide light and shade

Individual needs *and* behaviours
1. Makes statements that express own views – beginning with 'I' and not 'you'
2. Expresses feelings and thoughts or encourages others to express feelings and thoughts
5. Is assertive appropriately
6. Listens and helps others

When we consider the working of our own teams we will probably find that some of the positive behaviours that encourage effective team working are absent. To get these behaviours to occur in your team can now be one of your personal targets in improving your effectiveness as a manager.

Just as management and team style can be understood by considering the balance between the roles we prefer, so it is possible to understand that different managers seem to have totally different attitudes to their roles and their staff. Some people will accept without question my basic idea that a major role of the manager is to act as a facilitator, while others will see their roles as more active – 'A manager's job is to manage' – and probably involve constructs of leadership and military discipline. Other managers see themselves as inspirational, and others again as managing by example. These are all valid styles of management. Unfortunately, a refusal to accept that all styles have validity can produce communication blocks.

EXERCISE – A GENERAL MANAGER'S PROFILE

Here are six sets of views on management. You have ten points to distribute within each set. For instance, you could give all ten points to one statement which you feel completely reflects your views, or perhaps distribute the ten points more evenly. At the end of the exercise, you should have a total of 60 points in six batches of ten. There is no right or wrong view and the questions are intended to illustrate differences between effective managers in the field.

Score

1. My personal aim as a manager in an organisation is:

   a. To extend knowledge or understanding in my area
   b. To be useful
   c. To solve problems
   d. To keep the organisation on a moral basis

2. I am proud of:

   a. My staff or peers as people
   b. What we have/will have achieved
   c. Our abilities to solve problems
   d. My department or discipline

3. I feel we should be judged on:

   a. Our useful contacts
   b. The stimulus provided to the organisation
   c. Things that we have actually done which can be of use
   d. Our reputation as a centre of excellence

4. I get my personal job rewards from:

   a. Working with difficult problems
   b. Interacting with challenging people
   c. The respect from others doing similar things
   d. Sudden flashes of insight

5. I see my job as a people manager as:

   a. Making sure that 'good people' can be effective
   b. Developing their analytical skills
   c. Developing my people
   d. Maintaining a 'tight ship'

6. I think the best reports I produce:

a. Excite and stimulate my readers
b. Extend knowledge in some way
c. Clearly recommend courses of action
d. Present argued alternatives

When you have completed the form, score in the following way:

Section	WHY	WHAT	HOW	IF
1	d	a	c	b
2	a	d	c	b
3	b	d	a	c
4	b	c	a	d
5	c	b	d	a
6	a	b	d	c
TOTALS				

──────────────▶

You will remember the cycle of questions I used in Chapter 3 to structure the discussion on giving instructions and getting people to change their behaviour:

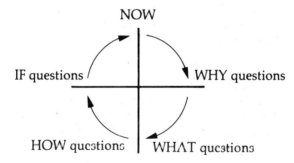

At the time, I said that different people needed different help round the cycle, and I discussed four case studies. The manager who was concerned with the *Why* questions was a highly creative computer systems architect and simply required to be motivated to ask *Why* questions by working from the previous sector (the *If* questions). The second manager was a chemical analyst by discipline and was an expert herself on *What* questions: for her to be started on the cycle, she needed to be supplied with the *Why* answers. The third manager was an engineer who liked working out the *How* answers provided that he was told *What* needed doing. The final character was a Market Researcher who needed to be given details of *How* her work was to be done, and would then complete the task without further control.

The four case studies are stereotypes of four types of manager with different views of their work and of their role. The questionnaire you have just completed may give you an inkling of your own view of work and of your role. Look at your scores and see how well the balance between the profiles I shall discuss fits you. It is unlikely that you will conform to one single profile, or that you will see yourself equally in all four portraits. As you read each profile, I should like you to think about several questions:

1. How well do I fit this profile?

2. Whom do I recognise that fits this profile?

3. What strengths and weaknesses could I or others see in someone who is *very* pronounced in this profile?

4. Where in my organisation would I be most likely to meet someone with this profile, and what would be the particular difficulties others with dissimilar profiles would find in communicating with them?

THE HIGH *WHY* PROFILE MANAGERS – THE IMAGINATIVES

Managers with a high *Why* profile, the *Imaginatives*, need to be personally involved with what they are doing – attempting to find meanings, clarity and integrity. They seek commitment in their staff and prefer to lead through participation and trust. They function through social interaction and learn by listening and sharing ideas. They can sometimes find themselves saying:

'I don't really know what I mean till I hear myself saying it.'

Imaginatives perceive through their own senses and are reflective, viewing reality through their own eyes, from ranging perspectives, and reaching several conclusions. They are divergent thinkers who are interested in people and culture as such. They model themselves on those they respect, and their goal in life is concerned with self-involvement and with bringing unity out of chaos.

The strength of the Imaginatives lies in their creativity and imagination, their ability to have new and different perspectives and ideas. Their weaknesses may lie in their 'fairness' and ability to see both sides of many questions. They may also be seen as slow in reaching action, as uncritical of their staff, and as being unable to 'see the trees for the wood'. They have certain favoured career paths which include primary school teaching, counselling, training, the humanities, corporate planning . . . wherever people or ideas are valued for their own sake.

As managers Imaginatives see themselves as facilitators who make the path smooth for others to act. They see staff appraisal in terms of motivation, and training in terms of personal growth. They can be quite vague on how they would like to be assessed themselves, but certainly it will be concerned with their impact on others.

The favourite question on the lips of the Imaginatives is, of course, Why?

THE HIGH *WHAT* PROFILE MANAGERS – THE LOGICS

Managers with a high What profile, the *Logics*, are more 'thing' people and seek facts and theories. They need to know what the experts think. They exert personal authority by assertive persuasion, until challenged, and then they are inclined to move into uncontrolled Critical Parent. As managers they are brave and protective, defending staff as a tiger with cubs.

They learn by thinking through ideas, and value sequential and ordered thinking, needing details to establish complete patterns. They are capable of forming a reality out of concepts, of collecting and assessing data, of re-examining them until fully understood. They can be seen as thorough and industrious, and they do well in traditional classroom situations. They function through models and by adapting to expert views. They are continuously exploring the '4 Ws' – What, Where, When, Who.

The strengths of the Logics arise from their concern with the detail of things and data, and from their ability to rise above the noise of people issues. As such they are often the record-keepers of groups and organisations, and prevent others from repeating mistakes. They are also well able to work alone.

The weaknesses of the Logics may relate to their wish to collect evidence as opposed to acting, and this can allow them to be seen as ponderous or even boring. They do not always acknowledge or even recognise when they or others come into dysfunctional stress. The careers in which Logics are found include the natural sciences, maths and computing, Research and Development, Planning, store-keeping . . .

As managers, Logics may see themselves as 'keeper of the keys',

as the guru who needs to protect his or her department from
outside contamination. I know of one R & D manager who had all
the characteristics I have described who told his staff not to answer
phone calls from the rest of the organisation '. . . as it might
disturb you from your work'.

The establishment of centres of professional excellence may
well be their view of the role of management and they judge
themselves and others in terms of order, efficiency, respect and
professionalism. They see appraisal as a way of rank-ordering
their departments, and training in terms of improving professional
skills.

THE HIGH *HOW* PROFILE MANAGERS – THE PRACTICALS

Managers with a high *How* profile, the *Practicals*, seek the
usability of everything they find. They need to know how things
work. They lead by inspiring a concept of 'best' in their group.
They learn by testing theoretical concepts for their application and
are concerned with gaining skills. They are the decision-makers
and are inclined to edit reality if, by that method, a difficult
decision can be made practicable. In human affairs, they can be
seen to use a hammer when perhaps a screwdriver might have been
preferable.

The Practicals enjoy solving problems and resent being given
answers. They resent the 'fuzzy' concept, and like to use factual
data to build on – often literally. Their strengths lie in practicalities
and their ability to work independently. They are good at evalua-
tion and detective work. They are good problem solvers, but may
be seen as bigoted by others.

The weaknesses of the Practicals lie in their single-mindedness
and lack of ability to be diverted: 'I've made up our mind – don't
bother me with more facts' has led to a few How-dominated
companies failing, including the British Rolls-Royce Company
before restructuring.

The career patterns of the How managers will involve the
practical world, with engineering in all its variations predominant
– asking 'How?' of the world in general.

As managers the Practicals act in the classic mould: they are the
resource controllers and they see their job as organising their staff
towards the task. They will also have had great difficulty with
many of the people-orientated concepts presented in this book.
Effectiveness is concerned with efficiency in performing the tasks
called for, and appraisal is concerned with certification. The

supreme test for a How manager is to look on his or her visiting
card. The How manager will have a string of initials after the
name. Training is concerned with conferring skills and often the
extreme How manager will link promotion to particular educa-
tional barriers set by training schemes.

THE HIGH *IF* PROFILE MANAGERS – THE *ENTHUSIASTS*

The managers I have termed Why, What and How are known as
the Imaginatives, the Logics and the Practicals. What I term the
high *If* profile managers are known also as the *Enthusiasts*. They
like doing things and often without due caution:

'Well you win some and lose some – what next?'

The Enthusiasts actually do things, anything. They seek hidden
possibilities and excitement, and need to know 'what things are
for' before they have any interest. They lead by energising, and
lose interest in those who refuse to be energised. They learn by
trial-and-error and self-discovery, and seek influence and solidar-
ity with others if necessary. They enrich reality, which may be
another way of saying that they exaggerate. They are adaptable to
and relish change and in extreme cases make 'flexibility into a bad
word'. They are at ease with people, but are often seen as pushy
and tire their companions. They could be seen as totally self-
centred. We can almost hear them say:

'I don't quite know what I'm going to do until I've done it'.

They also have the infuriating skill of reaching fairly accurate
conclusions on the flimsiest of evidence.

The Enthusiasts' strengths lie in their ability to make things
happen. Their weaknesses lie in not being particularly careful
about what things they make happen. Their likely careers are in
action-orientated management – often at the top of organisations,
in marketing, sales, management training . . .

As managers, the Enthusiasts perceive themselves as colleagues
and motivaters, but to the members of their staff not chosen for
the élite other words spring to mind, particularly during appraisal,
which the Enthusiasts see as an opportunity to weed out the non-
convinced. They like their staff to act 'independently', but since
planning and logical instruction-making are not their strong
points, this can be difficult. One head teacher who had identified
herself as a strong *If* profile manager once said to me:

'My idea of my job is to make sure the little swines have a

correctly packed knapsack for life. Once I see it's complete I want to kick them down the road and get on with the next batch.'

I have some sympathy for that terrible sentiment, because I am about 50% Enthusiast, 35% Imaginative and 15% Logic.

Obviously, taken at their extremes, the four categories of manager have difficulty in communicating. The Enthusiasts can be seen as 'bouncing' people, the Logics as 'boring', the Practicals as 'bigoted', and the Imaginatives as 'day-dreamers'. Unfortunately for us as individuals, but fortunately for the human race, we all have to live together. Look back on the questions I asked you to complete at the beginning of this section, and think where you will find the four types in quantity. How do you get over the communication blocks that thinking of others as 'day-dreamers', 'boring', 'bigoted' and 'totally self-centred' can bring about? You have enough information to identify your own difficulties, and to reach some effective plans for dealing with the blocks.

It may be interesting for the reader that David Kolb, who is responsible for a great number of my ideas on the cycle and personality styles of managers, also traced the careers of managers and showed that some career changes could be linked with personality styles at variance with the norm for the initially chosen profession.

An American worker has said:

> Many first marriages in the States are between people in opposite quadrants (*If* vs *What* or *Why* vs *How*) but most second marriages are with people from the same quadrant. This does not mean that second marriages are more successful – more that the rows are different.

I have no further comment. The next chapters will be concerned with the area outside your control – the organisation. I shall deal first with the classic organisations, and then with the new organisations that have appeared in response to the increasing rapidity of change in our world.

CHAPTER NINE

The New Manager Takes On the Organisation: Survival

'When I joined the organisation I knew where I was.'

'Information flow is always down, never up.'

'They *tell* me, but when it comes down to getting work out of my staff *telling* isn't the answer.'

'My staff have someone else to talk to, I haven't.'

'I seem to be in a sort of bottleneck: upstairs they talk to one another, below they negotiate. Me? . . . well, you tell me.'

In the last chapter, I discussed the world of the manager as being bounded by the organisation. The individual manager can do a great deal without resort to the organisation, and indeed may be penalised should the organisation notice his or her existence:

'In this group you get paid for making sure the job is done, and not for making waves.'

However, in all my collections of problem statements, issues of the manager and the organisation seem to generate maximum concern. This chapter deals with the way organisations evolve, and with the problems this evolution gives individual managers whose evolution in the workplace may not, even with prior notice, be at the same pace.

This book is not for academics but for managers in the field or, in this case, the organisation. The area of organisational communication is, in my view, one of the most controversial and most widely studied areas in Management Science; but the published information seems sadly lacking in the hard information a manager needs to survive, let alone grow. The theories and concepts behind the academic studies of organisations and their development are extremely difficult for managers to grasp in the time available and, perhaps more importantly, extremely difficult to relate to real here-and-now situations. This chapter is based on a method I have found successful in getting managers to look at their own organisations with sympathy, understanding and occasional flashes of insight. It will not satisfy the academic reader, but I make no apology.

---▶

EXERCISE

The organisations within which we work are the products of history. What has gone before has shaped the present, and it is a foolish manager who ignores this. Nobody has a clean slate.

Imagine you are a visitor to your own place of work. Come in from the street and describe how it feels.

Is there a formal entrance with a gate guard or can the visitor simply wander in?

Is the place spruce or tending towards the seedy?

What sort of reception do you get from the people you meet in the corridors? Do they smile or put their heads down and hurry on?

Are the office doors open or closed and is there an air of defeat or of confidence?

If you did not choose the Head Office for the wandering of your mind's eye, please move to the Head Office now.

Walk through reception, collect a visitor's badge if you have to, and hurry on up to the Executive Number 1 Conference Room which may be called variously the Directors' Room or the Boardroom. Look around and absorb the atmosphere.

------▶

The boardrooms of our organisations hold the key to the past and the way the organisations view the present. The reception area may be crammed with new technology, but if the boardroom is still walnut and oil paintings, then believe the boardroom. The New Manager, if he or she is ever to grow into management, needs to understand that the most sophisticated communications from any organisation have to match the style of the boardroom and that, when the pressures are really on, every message is filtered through its walls, however much has been invested in high technology networking. A tradition-soaked panelled room encourages a tradition-soaked leadership style, but a room doubling with the Training department and Marketing for sales display encourages something quite different. I have met one such boardroom in a company struggling after a management buy-out. It acted as the Conference Room and the Managing Director's office, and doubled as a showroom for the office furniture that was the company's staple product. Nobody in that company mistook the 'all in it together' management style of that company.

The custodian of the boardroom style is the Chief Executive and, because of the way organisations are built, we need to understand the 'style' before we can understand communications in real organisations. I know managers who have attempted to work against the style of the organisation, or indeed the style of the Chief Executive, either accidentally or deliberately. It doesn't work, and very often they have found themselves not working either.

Let's start by looking at the way in which organisations are built, and incidentally, at the role of the Chief Executive. I am going to ask you to help with the development of New World Holdings Group (previously trading as Bloggs Industries PLC, and initially as J. Bloggs Ltd).

---------►

EXERCISE

Imagine yourself as consultant to Mr Bloggs, J.P., Chairman and founder of J. Bloggs Ltd. Mr Bloggs wishes to set up new factories and is requesting help with the organisational detail. Read his words and attempt to see the man behind them.

MEMORANDUM

From: Mr J. Bloggs, J.P.   To: Reader Consultants Ltd
Chairman, J. Bloggs Ltd

Dear Mr Reader,

Your company has been recommended to me by a colleague on the Bench. I am shortly to construct a factory in an area new to industry. The construction makes sound economic sense provided labour costs are kept to a minimum. The demand for my products, with sound control of costs, should remain high. I would remind you that the production in all my factories is labour-intensive and will remain so.

It is my intention to use as many of the local people in the factory as possible and I would like your assistance in drawing up guidelines for the organisation, control and management of the factory, covering the following points:

1. Job Design. How should work be allocated to the workforce to guarantee delivery times and quality?

2. Organisation Design. What sort of structure would you recommend to maintain continuous and satisfactory production?

3. Management Style. How must the factory be managed?

4. Control and Communication. What would you recommend to fit the Job and Organisational Design already recommended?

5. Reward systems. What form of reward and payment systems would you recommend – Piece Rate, Group Bonus, Flat Rate or Incentive schemes?

Before making your recommendations I would refer you to a confidential report from the previous consultants, a report that was instrumental in my choosing this particular site.

'The workforce of the area is non-unionised, ignorant of industrial work practices and materially impoverished. Their lifestyle affords ample opportunity for idleness and often intemperance which, allied to their history of independence and disunity, represents their basic characteristics.'

I expect your report on my desk within the next week.

Yours faithfully,

J. Bloggs.

When I look at the replies I have had from dozens of groups of managers set the exercise of the first memorandum, I find a common thread. Very few indeed are basic enough. In the West, we have become soaked in the 'fancy trappings' that Mr Bloggs will reject as being unnecessary if not actually dangerous. We have begun to see these 'fancy trappings' as essentials. For example, the reports from the consultants have contained welfare schemes which resulted in the following reply:

'Look lads, this is my money and we will have none of that. They can look after themselves, and if they get into trouble they can go back from whence they came.'

I have had suggested joint-consultation and even safety committees, but Mr Bloggs will have none of them. To him, these are simply examples of the multitude of ways his softer competitors have been dragged into increasing overheads. Mr Bloggs will get most angry if we dare to suggest that such ideas will 'prevent trouble in the future'. He sees his universe very simply, and any comment against his construction will be seen as a criticism and a challenge. Mr Bloggs is the complete Critical Parent manager, and any attempt on our part to get him to be a Nurturing Parent by moving towards Logic and Adult will be rejected. The archetypal Critical Parent manager gives himself away in his letter and warns us to stay in line. He wants Adapted Child in us, just as in his managers, supervisors and workforce. What particular words and phrases are we discussing that give Mr Bloggs' game away? Well:

'. . . makes sound economic sense provided labour costs are kept to a minimum.'

'. . . is labour-intensive and will remain so.'

and of course, his endorsement of the wording from the previous consultant's report:

'Their lifestyle affords ample opportunity for idleness and often intemperance.'

Before we answer the questions in the memorandum in a way that will be acceptable to Mr Bloggs, we ought to look at our own position should we happen to work for any Critical Parent manager in the mould of Bloggs.
Information flows down. We have an image of Mr Bloggs, and indeed many of the great industrialists who founded our world, as marching through their factories with their managers in tow, like

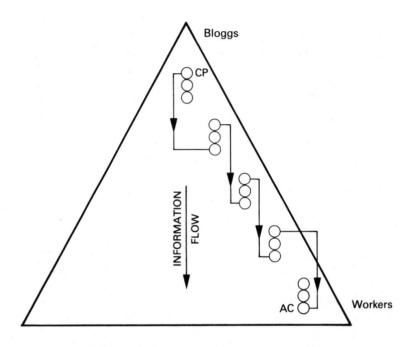

some ogre surgeon with his housemen. Every so often he will pause to hand out his tablets of stone and we, his managers, will gratefully take the instructions and pass them on to our supervisors. According to the Berne model of Transactional Analysis, we can see Mr Bloggs as the Critical Parent and ourselves as Adapted Child accepting the orders. Because we cannot question (the Adapted Child can only rebel) we have to pass the orders on in such a way as to avoid being so questioned ourselves. Our reason for disliking being questioned is simply that, since we have no possibility for manoeuvre, we cannot allow our subordinates any space either. It is the same down the line. The Critical Parent manager forces all those below to adopt the same management style. No questioning down the line means that communication must be downward only. Bloggs' construct of the universe is complete, in his eyes, and therefore he has no need to find out what the others think. If they do not understand, they are fools; if they do not agree they are wrong; in either case, *sack them*.

How, then, would he arrange his organisation (on our advice of course)? The questions are fundamental to any organisation and begin with *Job Design* – the way we would specify what needs to be done.

There is a spectrum in Job Design – of job specifications – ranging from the general, 'See what you can do to reduce defects on the line', to the detailed, 'Take the nut from the bin and place it on the spindle'. In Mr Bloggs' new factory we are towards the detailed end of the spectrum: each job will be tightly controlled, and will probably be the subject of careful workstudy. There will be rigid inspection systems, and bad workmanship will be penalised.

The *Organisational Design* will be structured in such a way as to make possible the detail of the Job Design. A single gaffer, Mr Bloggs, will employ a minimum of administrative staff and managers to oversee 'the production side of the business'. We will have a classical pyramid structure, and the number of staff in each area will depend on the precise nature of the product and the degree of inspection needed to maintain quality. I have met simple technologies – for example, the manual stripping of chicken to make pies – where one supervisor was responsible for 200 workers. I have met order-picking workers where the level of supervision was nearer one to ten. Whatever the ratio, the jobs will be clearly defined, both for the floor-worker and the supervisor.

There will be no Personnel or Training departments:

'I want no parasites in my organisations.'

The *Management Style* will be clear and authoritarian. The low administration costs Mr Bloggs demands can be met only by a 'telling' management style, expressed in the tone of the original memorandum. Mr Bloggs does not trust the workforce and will take advantage of their non-unionisation. The Critical Parent of Mr Bloggs – by nature, as we have said before, authoritarian – will address the Adapted Child in his managers – a fact that we would have found to our cost had we pressed for a more enlightened style of management. Since the head man is a Critical Parent figure, and we are not in a position to discuss our orders from him (Adapted Children don't discuss, they either obey or rebel), we in turn have no alternative but to adopt the same Critical Parent style towards our staff. Since we have no room to negotiate, we cannot allow those in our charge the luxury either. So it goes down the line: our supervisors meet us as Adapted Child and meet the workforce as Critical Parent; they, too, have the choice to rebel or obey, and become Critical Parent Supervisors. The progression, the sequence Critical Parent to Adapted Child down the line, is inevitable simply because nobody within the organisation below

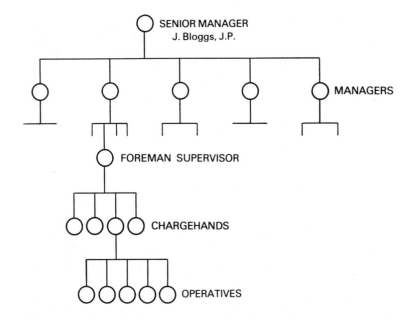

Bloggs himself has any freedom of action, or is privy to any information beyond that essential to his or her job.

If any manager or supervisor or foreman attempted a consultative approach, he or she would lose credibility.

'Is it OK for us to finish tomorrow, there is nothing else due in?'

This is a perfectly Adult request which the consultative manager would have enough information to process. In our case, working for Bloggs, we would not have enough information, only the fact that we were told to complete the packing. The unwise might say:

'I'm afraid I do not know Mr Bloggs' plans, so you'd better get on with it.'

But the wise person is much more likely to say:

'This job has to be completed today.'

The issue of the manager in the authoritarian chain was most potently expressed by a woman I once met surviving successfully in just such an organisation as that of Mr Bloggs. She told me that she treated all her staff as zombies. I asked her how her boss treated her:

'As a zombie, of course.'

The *Control and Communication* in the authoritarian organisation must be tight and severe, to reduce the likelihood of too many rebellious Adapted Children. Since we begin by trusting nobody, we have to live with the consequences. Adults can be negotiated with over a range of subjects, from work times to quality standards. Adapted Children need to be told and to be monitored and to be punished for deviation. I have a vision of a notice in an old woollen mill:

> All supervisors are reminded that the work is dull and repetitious and will not afford any satisfaction. Any misdemeanours must be dealt with promptly according to the scale of fines below.

Mr Bloggs will hope to hear, throughout his factory, from all his staff, managers and workers: 'I'm not paid to think.' Communication will come from Mr Bloggs through his managers, and he will not expect to hear any messages coming up from lower levels. Mr Bloggs will be perfectly happy with his lack of what we might call feedback, because he will deny the importance of knowing what *they* think or want. They, and you his manager, are paid to do a job, and if they or you don't like it, then there is a clear alternative.

The *Reward System* must be compatible with the driving concepts of the organisation. It is likely to be a piece-work system, with penalties for bad work and a 'hire and fire' policy.

The Critical Parent/Authoritarian organisation is very efficient and created the modern industrial world – its successes and its scars. It can be seen in undiluted form in many Third World operations, and perhaps surprisingly in many plants in Russia. It built the pyramids and it builds the Lada car.

For all its efficiency, it has certain weaknesses that make it unstable. The Canadian slate industry owes its sudden growth in the early twentieth century to a fatal strike in the North Wales mines. The owner pushed his Critical Parent's role on the workforces too far, and did not recognise the real complaints of his workforce. The Adapted Children flipped into rebellion, and stayed there to destroy the entire industry by a strike that spanned the First World War. The folly that converted a major industry into an industrial museum has been echoed many times, and will continue to be echoed.

A second issue is perhaps more subtle than the flip from Adapted to Rebellious Child, and is concerned with the nature of

the task. A Critical Parent organisation can function only when
the task is clear. If the task is ill-defined, if it cannot be laid down
with precision or take account of changes, then the Critical Parent
organisation is shaken. In our example, Mr Bloggs knew every
nut, every nuance of the process from raw material to customer.
Because he knew all about everything, he did not need to listen. He
did not need feedback because his real instruction was, 'Do the
same . . . harder . . . faster . . . more'. If the technology changed
without his being in total command of the new skills, or if any
single aspect of the process demanded so much of his skills or time
as meant that real delegation was necessary, then the whole edifice
of the Critical Parent organisation would begin to crumble. The
residue of such happenings lingers in the walnut of boardrooms
and in the oil paintings of past Chairmen.

The Benevolent Organisation

The concept of clear, authoritarian management and a compliant
workforce may be convenient at the beginning of the industrialisa-
tion process, but in fact it disappears quite fast. Several of the
nineteenth-century entrepreneurs made significant movements to
maintain the compliant workforce by providing isolation. It
would be unfair to look at the model villages of Lever's at Port
Sunlight, of Cadbury's and Dunlop's near Birmingham, of Salt's
near Bradford, or indeed of any of the others, as merely negative
ways of isolating a workforce from the virus of self-interest. There
was a very positive background to these contributions to improving worker conditions. The Critical Parent organisation was being
replaced by Nurturing Parent systems.

Looking at the Memorandum from Mr Bloggs, we notice the
consultants' phrase, 'history of independence and disunity', and
we realise that this is the starting-point only. As people work
together, the very act of common purpose destroys both independence and disunity. Groups form, and groups have a life of their
own. All Mr Bloggs is doing with his authoritarian rule is to push
the Role and Control issues underground.

I have already discussed how Joining and Belonging to groups,
the satisfaction from so belonging, is a human characteristic; and
however disunited or undeveloped a group may be at the beginning, force them together and they will unite. In order to Join and
Belong to the group, the individual will soon take on some of the
group norms and suppress some of his or her ambitions. During

the process of individual adaptation, the issues of the task in hand – of the task as defined by Mr Bloggs and his ilk – are nowhere. The group norms may be expressed in dress or in more subtle forms of behaviour. It is not an accident that the college lecturer and the IBM executive can be readily distinguished at the airport. The more subtle behaviours were first discussed in connection with what is known as the Hawthorne Experiment, in a study of female workers of the Westinghouse Brake Company.

Westinghouse wanted to know whether changes in the working environment would affect the efficiency of assembly workers in one of their plants. They hired a team from Harvard to study how production efficiency would be affected if the heating, the lighting and the noise levels were changed: and they found that they were. The method was to compare the production efficiency of paired rooms. The first room was left alone as a control and the second room had the environmental changes. As the men from Harvard changed the lighting, up went the production. As they changed the heating, up went the production. In fact, whatever they changed in the experimental rooms, up went the production. When, in desperation, they put all the conditions in the experimental rooms back to the original levels, they still found that *productivity in the test rooms remained above that of the unobserved control units.* Panic in the research team.

In the cold light of reflection they deduced that two things had happened, both of which have had a profound effect on the organisation of factories ever since. The first was that the women were able to set their own work-rates by informal agreements, and perhaps against the interests of particularly talented or motivated individuals. The group set norms of behaviour, and the group members stuck to these in a behaviour which amounted to conspiracy. The work-rates and the bonuses at Westinghouse had been carefully developed by workstudy methods, so the fact that observed rates bore little relationship to the 'real' rates may indicate that 'conspiracy' is not too strong a word. We can visualise the individual woman chosen to be observed by the Work Study Engineers as judging her performance very carefully, and her judgement being even more carefully monitored through very detailed negotiations with her fellows. The negotiations, of which management knew nothing, would have arranged it so that the standard rate of production, calculated by the workstudy engineers from observations of the chosen worker, would be low enough for all but the very weakest workers to achieve a bonus in time of need, but high enough to allay suspicion. The chosen worker would have to perform this masterly piece of histrionics in order to remain in the group, and regardless of whether it was in her own personal interests. Once the standard rate of production had been published, the women would determine how hard each member of the group worked so that the special needs of the group and individuals for bonus money could be met on occasion, but not so frequently that the standard rate would be raised. The discipline and organisation this called for was regarded by the Harvard workers as remarkable. We now understand that the group had become mature outside the management structure. It had developed past the Joining and Belonging needs, and had fully established its own parallel Role and Control structure. The Pairing and Sharing was complete. The desire to satisfy the human contact needs in the group had overridden not only any individual needs but also the accuracy techniques of the previously unchallenged 'scientific' methods of Work Study.

The second thing that was adjudged to have happened came from looking at the 'conspiracy' – the product of the unofficial mature group within the building but outside the company's organisation. Work people had got together in a group, without the blessing of management, and had actually done something. No amount of looking at the organisation charts in Westinghouse would have discovered the informal organisation that had determined the preferred working norms of the group, and enforced loyalty. A complete underground mechanism of rewards and penalties and hierarachies allowed the bonus to increase enough to pay for Christmas, but not enough for anyone in management to be suspicious. It allowed individuals in need to earn more, and curbed those it felt unworthy.

The sub-organisation that existed and was identified in Westinghouse is known as the *Informal Workgroup*, and its creation is a universal process in any official organisation once the physiological needs of hunger and survival have been satisfied, and people have established their own pattern of Joining and Belonging, Role and Control and finally Pairing and Sharing, despite organisational hostility or indifference. Because the pattern of deriving human satisfaction from work has been developed in spite of the organisation in our informal workgroups, it is unlikely that they function for the good of the organisation, and occasionally they can be quite bizarre.

My own first workplace made equipment on a cost-plus basis for the British Government. The production was literally controlled by a small inner group who played poker during the meal breaks. The poker players were able to move both bonus payments and overtime demands to compensate for personal financial losses during the very flexible 'rest' periods. The weight of what I will call euphemistically the 'personality' of the inner group was such that, in our months working in the factory, no management was ever seen on the shopfloor. The supervision had long since given up the unequal struggle, and when the ill-negotiated Government contract ended, so did the factory, informal and formal structures together.

———————▶

EXERCISE

Take your own organisation and list the 'informal' groups that exist outside the formalised organisation charts.

Include in your list such informal groups as 'Friday-lunch-drink-at-the-pub' groups who arrange for flexible manning on Fridays. Include 'pools syndicates', 'baby sitting circles', 'mail order clubs', and the closed or semi-closed religious, political or status-based societies. Add to these the semi-formal groups of unions and social and welfare committees.

In your list you will probably find that the groups have survived across time. Thus, the Friday lunch group may well span several departments now that its members have moved in the organisation. You may also see that they provide an informal communication system and account for much of the grapevine.

Look hard at the informal groups and recognise the good and bad points from the standpoint of the organisation. Overall, is the contribution of each particular contribution to the informal power structure of the organisation good or bad?

———————▶

From my experience, I would guess that there is a very sophisticated informal power base within your organisation which owes more to individual than to organisational survival.

How was the conspiracy of the informal workgroup broken in the Hawthorne Experiment at Westinghouse? The unravelling of the mechanism was very important for the future of industrial organisations, and derived from the nature of the experiment itself. Imagine what it was like for women working in a boring job suddenly to be the centre of interest for a group of young male college graduates. Suddenly people, and good-looking people at that, were interested in them and the way they worked. The women were being recognised, and rose to the situation by performing well. For the first time they were being noticed, and they were being motivated in the workplace by such notice.

After the Hawthorne Experiment, management theorists began to realise that informal workgroups existed and were important. They began to understand the secondary advantage of the industrial villages of Lever, Cadbury, Dunlop and Salt in that they provided a focus for, or control of, the energies of the informal workgroups. If they exist anyway, then let's get them on our side.

The management advisers also decided that it was possible to institutionalise human recognition. The 'Hello Dolly' school of supervision was born, and with it the Nurturing Parent became the flavour of the organisational month.

————▶

EXERCISE

How would you answer the following?

From: Sir John Bloggs   To: Reader Consultants Ltd

Dear Mr Reader,

Bloggs Industries PLC has come a long way since I first called upon the services of your company, and although your fees were exorbitant, what you suggested was sound.

I have recently become disturbed that things are not right in the factories. I cannot put so much time into my inspections, and in fact they are now weekly and not daily, but this is not the point. Production is falling off and so is quality.

I hear from my son who is at College – Cambridge, of course – that my management style – whatever that means – is old-fashioned. Basically, I am used to barking and expect them to do what I want, and I am not going to change now.

Production is less than I know they can do. Competition is

up, and the net result is that we are beginning to lose money.

You are up with the latest things. What can I do – remembering that I still think a manager's job is to manage? Give me some ideas that will work, sound ideas.

Yours faithfully . . .

Note: I think young Mr Bloggs has been reading something about the Hawthorne Experiment, so you had better mention that in your report.

Mrs Ferguson (Secretary)

Copy to Sir John

————————▶

If we look at the informal workgroup we can see it fulfilling the basic human need of human contact. The whole concept behind the original Critical Parent organisation was one of exploitation of a faceless workforce of non-cohesive cyphers. What Sir John Bloggs is asking us is how to marry the concept of a workforce having an internal cohesion with the desire to keep them in Adapted Child. There is a real and often proven justifiable fear that cohesion may lead to that worst of all industrial plagues, organised rebellion. Without the benefit of the Hawthorne Experiment, the fathers of industry recognised that workers consisted of family groups, of groups with common interests and common religions. In their villages they built social centres, halls, churches and schools. The men of Lever's Port Sunlight might want to meet together, so the best place for them to meet was the Lever Club, and the best thing they could do was to win a cup at the Lever Sports Club. Their children went to the Lever School and borrowed books from the Lever Library, while their mothers met at the Port Sunlight Mothers' Union. The groups were encouraged to perform excellently and out-perform workers of lesser firms. The Critical Parent showed occasionally in that no alcohol was allowed to be sold in the original village; but overall the effect was patriarchal, caring and in our language, an effective Nurturing style. The workforce was looked after from birth to death, and rewarded the company by a loyalty that endures to this day.

So how do we reply to Sir John Bloggs? Building a workers' industrial village might be a little expensive, but he could certainly afford a Bloggs Works Brass Band. He could ensure that families were cared for and perhaps, when little Maisie – the daughter of Bill in the carpenter's shop – was ill, let her rest in a Bloggs-dedicated bed in the local hospital. For good workers, he could perhaps convert his piece-work systems to hourly pay with group bonus. There could be departmental safety awards and house-keeping prizes, even a Newsheet to mark achievements in production and marketing and high scores at darts.

Job Design would have to remain strong and clear for the shop floor, but at supervisory level and upward, discretion could be allowed. Our latest memorandum would have to encourage training for the supervisory staff to recognise the workforce as individuals, and probably get them to say 'Hello' to Dolly every morning. If recognising Dolly as an individual meant giving some sympathy to her private problems, that would be fine. Occasionally, a particularly deserving Dolly could be recorded in the Newsheet.

The Organisational Design would remain the same as before for management and supervisory staff and the multiple canteens would symbolise it – a directors' dining-room, a white-coat dining-room and a works canteen being the minimum class divisions the organisation would need. Below the supervisory level, we might recommend a series of committees to deal with sports and social activities and welfare. In our reply to Sir John, we would be wise to recommend that the chairman of each committee be a senior manager, and that the terms of reference be very clear, so that welfare did not in any sense stretch to Terms and Conditions of Employment. We might in our wisdom know that we were planting the seeds of consultation, but we would be clear that the seeds should not be allowed to germinate.

The Management Style of our recommended organisation might variously be called Benevolent or Nurturing, but it is clear that it does not seek to use the potential of the workers as people. They are still expected to hang their brains on the hatstand when they clock in, and the job of the manager is still to manage. The organisation, by taking the move from Critical to Nurturing, has attempted to convert a threat into an opportunity.

Remember our mind's eye view of our own organisation, what might we expect to find in a Nurturing organisation? We would expect to have a panelled boardroom and a covering of oil paintings, but also various certificates for safety awards. In the corridors we would expect to find staff notice boards, and a member of administration would make sure that they were carefully cleared of 'subversive' material. Coach trips would be announced and local theatres would proclaim their products. There would be several canteens, divided by grade, and there would be a Personnel and Training department.

The final test of a Nurturing organisation is the same as for a Critical Parent organisation. Communication, except in 'welfare matters', is still downward. Both organisations are designed for the Parent to Child chain of command, and everyone knows his or her place when things come to a head.

I would say that the formality of information flow and its general downward direction are both the strength and the fatal flaw in both the Critical Parent and the Nurturing Parent organisation. In a changing world, organisations need to be able to react, and it is sensible that they hear from the readiest as well as the most loyal information source of all – their own employees. Without that information, their reactions will be unnecessarily slow.

The problems of the Nurturing Parent organisation become most acute in connection with Control and Communication at the supervisor level. Basically, the objectives of the workforce are the same as before, and therefore the objectives of the supervisor are the same. The work has to be got out at the right price, time and quality. Above the supervisor, there are the rumblings of consultation. The supervisor's boss may be on a committee that hears things ahead of the supervisor, and certainly his or her subordinates will begin to understand things about senior management that the supervisor is not able to defend or even understand. The discussion on welfare will inevitably involve areas on the fringes of the job. These fringe areas are not challenges to management, but may trample on the authority of foreman, chargehand and supervisor. They will inevitably be bypassed. The contacts of the new committees will involve levels of management from which they are excluded. They may hear about changes in the workplace *after* they have become common knowledge on the factory floor. The supervisor grades may also feel, rightly, threatened by individuals on the shop floor who find the 'stamp of approval' coming from their presence on various committees, thus providing an alternative ladder to promotion. The worker – night school – chargehand – foreman route has been broken.

Perhaps the bitterest pill of all is that there seems no equivalent to 'Hello Dolly' for the supervisor from management. The concept of 'other ranks' still marks out the supervisor from the 'officer class'. This last comment may reflect a purely British disease, but such a relationship occurs in some form in many cultures. The supervisor has also lost both a carrot and a stick of control. Nurturing Parent is a weaker style of communication than the bowler-hatted Critical Parent of the old organisation. Lines are blurred; and when Dolly cries, the supervisor may know the reason, a problem not known in the old organisation, where everyone knew their place and the consequences of forgetfulness. The old-style supervisor also had the carrot of favours, but these are the very areas controlled by the committees.

Should Benevolent Management fail to stem the informal groups, the issues of unionisation begin. Unionisation brings a new world to both the supervisor and the manager.

If we put the clock forward and allow Bloggs Industries to live in the turbulent world of rapid changes of public taste, of waves of foreign competition, of movements in exchange rates, of new technologies and increasing rates of obsolescence – in skills, products and materials – neither of the Parent organisations can hope to survive. We need to establish communications where at least some of the workforce is able to contribute more than a pair of hands, and heads are not 'left on the hatstand'. We need to establish workgroups that are concerned with the task and not simply, as were the informal workgroups, with establishing human needs. Some years ago, I would have discussed the Maslow or even the Marxist organisational plan, but now the field is much wider and, perhaps for Western eyes, widened by the Japanese management principles.

------▶

EXERCISE

What factors have you observed in your own organisation that are not, or could not, be held by either of the Parent-Child structures?

Your list is likely to be long, complex and unique.

------------▶

In the next chapter, I shall discuss the range of responses that the challenges have brought and how you, the New Manager, will feel the wind of change.

CHAPTER TEN

The New Manager Takes On the Organisation: Growth

'I've been told the theories of Taylor, Mayo, Maslow, Marx and even the Japanese. Life is simply not like that.'

'I've been told that I have to be a consultative manager – *told* mind you.'

'We seem to spend all our time consulting.'

'I work in what they call a matrix – fine for the first year, but now I seem to have lost all contact with the people for whom I have line responsibility.'

'We try everything – somebody goes on a course and we try it.'

'We used to have a sort of club atmosphere here; it was nice. Now it's "all change" all the time.'

'The retirement age will be before we join soon.'

In the last chapter, we found ourselves with three major issues that put the Parent organisations under threat when faced with change:

Communications. In the Parent organisations, communications are inevitably top-down.

Diverging group loyalty. The informal workgroups that form in any organisation have developed to fulfil basic human needs, and are not in any way related to the task the organisation wishes to pursue.

'When you come into the factory you are expected to hang your brain on the company hatstand.' The Parent organisations were simply not using the human resource efficiently.

Peters and Waterman, in their book *In Search of Excellence,* quote

'The General Motors Poem' which to my mind spells out the death
of the Parent organisations in a nice way:

> Are these men and women
> Workers of the World?
> or is it an outgrown nursery
> with children – goosing, slapping, boys
> giggling, snotty girls?
> What is it about the entrance way,
> those gates to the plant? Is it the
> guards, the showing of your badge – the smell?
> is there some invisible eye
> that pierces you through and
> transforms your being? Some aura
> or ether, that brain and spirit washes you
> and commands, 'For eight hours
> you shall be different.'
> What is it that instantaneously makes
> a child out of a man?
> Moments before he was a father, a husband,
> an owner of property,
> a voter, a lover, an adult.
> When he spoke at least some listened.
> Salesmen courted his favour.
> Insurance men appealed to his family responsibility
> and by chance the church sought his help . . .
> But that was before he shuffled past the guard,
> climbed the steps,
> hung up his coat and
> took his place along the line.

The Parent organisations were places that made 'a child out of a
man' and could afford to be so as long as their total eco-system
allowed it. The changes that allowed the General Motors worker
to be heard, and quoted in probably the most respected management book of the decade, were changes in society, combined with
changes in technology. The problem for the individual manager,
as expressed by the problem statements at the beginning of the
chapter, is the confusion of solutions offered in response to the
changes resulting from the pressures on the old Parent-based
organisations becoming too great.

Corporate Man erects organisations to perpetuate the present,
be it in Staff Lists or in bricks and mortar. The old organisations,
whatever their failings, had a robust simplicity. The Bloggs

dynasty defined its own position and, in so doing, defined the position of each and every person in its employment: there were no Role and Control conflicts in Bloggs factories. The seas of turbulence that moved many of our workplaces to the confusions they now find themselves in produced the new organisational theories and experiments, but Corporate Man still sought a return to the old robust simplicity. Corporate Man wanted one solution that fitted all parts of his organisation and, in some cases, all organisations. With this in mind, the Adult organisation was developed and with it came the magic word *consultation*. The pure Adult organisation, if it ever existed, was only short-lived, because Corporate Man ignored the side-effects of attempting to involve the Adult in a workforce. Corporate Man forgot that the Adult in each and every one of us differs. Corporate Man forgot that, once all employees became more than a cypher, individual differences needed to be catered for, or, to put it in slogan form, 'He who is told to act consultatively must be consulted.' Consultation is not a process caught once and for all in a snapshot. It is a process whose limits are difficult to define and remain a subject for individual conjecture.

Consultative organisation

I was asked to consider with the entire management team of a factory the issues that would surround conversion to a 'Single Status' organisation. The factory was distinctly in the Parent organisation stage, with strong similarities to Bloggs' first ideas. The concept of 'Single Status' came from Head Office and was intended to enable the company to survive the massive changes taking place in the industry.

The practicalities of Single Status working involved losing the time clock and the separated dining facilities. All established employees were to have similar conditions of work, and piece-work would go. The detail was vast and in consulting the managers I divided them into sub-groups to study the issue from the point of view of particular categories of employee – from the board to part-time cleaners. The final report of the sub-groups was presented quite light-heartedly in role – for instance, the group studying the cleaners' issues spoke as if they were actually middle-aged ladies who communicated among themselves in Polish. The whole presentation, which at best showed luke-warm support for the idea of Single Status, was put on video.

A short time afterwards, the company controlling the factory announced that Single Status working would begin in the next week and no further consultation would take place. As one of the managers said: 'I've been told to be a consultative manager - *told* mind you.' She was not very happy.

The point of this true story is not that one attempt at a move towards consultation, expressed as a Single Status organisation, is good or bad. It was simply one company's response to its specific problems in its adaptation to the new and frightening world within which it now has to operate. The point of the story is that the Single Status organisation was adopted partly as a route to a Consultative organisation, although those were not the words the management would have used. They felt that communication was being hindered by the traditional class structure of their organisa-tion, and they saw more effective working systems operated by their competitors. They felt that the easier flow of information up, down and across in the Single Status organisation could not but help adaptation to change. The company decided to adopt the Single Status organisation system, whose principle claim to con-sideration is consultation, without carrying through the consulta-tive process with its own managers. Consultation cannot be imposed. By imposing consultation they ignored its serious side effect: once people have been consulted and accepted that they are being heard, it is profoundly dangerous to stop listening to them.

The managers, when they were consulted and before the decision was imposed, had discovered that the change to Single Status would involve effort, and effort in a real organisation costs money. Any form of organisation restructuring gives problems and involves cost in time, effort and often hard cash. In this case, the managers had identified how that effort could best be struc-tured for success. Their view that the effort was probably not outweighed by the advantages had to be taken account of, once it had been articulated. The problem the company had was that the senior management still saw themselves as a Parent organisation whose 'job was to manage' while being drawn towards the practices of a Consultative organisation, which must listen, balance and communicate. If Single Status is imposed, the net gain will be considerably reduced, and perhaps lost altogether.

What are the issues that make managers abandon the organisatio-nal security of the Parent organisations and move into the uncharted waters of the various forms of the Consultative organisation? The answers were hinted at in previous chapters, but maybe we ought to let Mr Bloggs Jnr explain the issues facing his organisation. As usual, he will explain in the family tradition of a letter to the reader.

MEMORANDUM

From: Mr Bloggs Jnr.   To: Reader Consultants Ltd

Dear Sir or Madam,

As you may have heard from your many contacts with my father, I have just returned from the States and am now equipped to take on what we used to call the 'family business'. I would like your help again to advise our organisation on how to proceed.

The original factory has of course been drastically altered but many of the old buildings and traditions linger on. We have just completed a massive redundancy programme to trim our workforce – white as well as blue collar – to meet the new demands of modern techniques and markets. Our remaining workforce is much more skilled and technically competent. It is also much younger and sophisticated. The most highly skilled also know their own market value and recruitment and retainment is difficult. They lack the basic loyalty of my Grandfather's day and their mobility is a great problem, not only to new and more custom built factories in the locality but also to our competitors, many of whom are abroad. Knowing what some of them do is also a problem.

I find myself looking back increasingly to the 'Good Old Days' when management was relatively easy and everyone knew his or her place. One could establish a hospital or a library for the workforce and they were grateful. Now they expect a private health schcmo to provide facilities that would be inconceivable for our old Cottage Hospital and the video library at the Leisure Centre is convenient when they finish their game of squash. Grandfather gave them an unheated swimming pool and some grass and they were grateful. The County gives them an Olympic Bath and a floodlit sports stadium within easy motoring distance.

Even if internally I could halt change, the market spurs me on. Our products are now subject to rapid swings of fashion and I cannot afford to distance myself from the market. The 'in phrase' is 'Get Close to the Customer', and that my Grandfather ceased to do many years ago. I know my salespersons are close to the customer but I am distant from my salespersons. I know my workers actually are

customers, but I have no way of hearing what they say. I have no
means of technical, design, financial or commercial flexibility without unduly straining my organisation.

Quality is a problem and I feel supervision lies at the root. Our
products are becoming increasingly complex and the cost of rejects
is spiralling. I feel that we must make things correctly first time and
not waste time, money and materials in rejects. I also feel that only
the workers have the understanding to make things correctly first
time and asking supervisors to take over this responsibility is
asking for the impossible. I would like your help in suggesting how I
should proceed.

J. Bloggs Jnr, Managing Director

New Industries PLC (formally trading as Bloggs Industries plc)
part of the New World Holdings Group

As usual, the current member of the Bloggs family has diagnosed
many of the problems in his organisation. Some years ago, I
would simply have waved the magic banners of Self-Actualisation
and Communication and retired to a tax haven to count my
consultancy fees. In the late eighties I have to work a little harder;
but before I do that, perhaps I had better explain what the magic
banners represented. In Chapter 4, I mentioned the work of
Maslow and his concept of a 'hierarchy of needs'. Put into this
context, Maslow would see the Parent organisations as providing
all but the pinnacle of human needs, what he called Self-Actualisation. The baser needs of the body, for food and shelter, were
satisfied as was once recognised – the need for belonging to a
group. The need for esteem and status was carefully catered for by
giving people coats or hats of different colours, canteens of
different service levels, and in later days, different standards of
car. What was not done was to allow the personal development of
the individual – Self-Actualisation. The Parent organisations
expected individuality to be hung on the hatstand on entry and to
be collected on leaving.

The secret of Self-Actualisation was seen to be two-way communication – using the Adult in the workforce. Managers had to
understand their instructions and explain them to the workforce.
The workforce had to be given sufficient information about the
job to be able to understand justifiable instructions. Thus organisations had to consult and inform: they had to treat their

employees as complete human beings, and accept that the whole needs of individuals were to be catered for. In the terms of Transactional Analysis, the new organisations took in the Adult, the Parent and all the Child states when they took on an employee, and not just the Adapted Child. The new organisations took on the responsibility for personal growth. Three assumptions were made: people wanted their place of work to take on joint responsibility for their personal growth; Self-Actualised people worked more effectively; and everyone wanted to be concerned with the task. Looking back on the concept, I would like to challenge all of these sweeping assumptions. Even at the highest levels of intellect they do not fit my own observations.

In my post-graduate class, I had two students who were outstanding. One arrived exactly at 09.00 each day and worked steadily till 17.00, when he packed his bags and left. He made no effort to join in any of the activities of his fellow students, and presented an excellent and original PhD on time. The other student practically lived in the laboratory. He worked all hours and joined in everything that was going. His heart and soul were in the work of the Department, and after he had completed, again well and on time, he was sadly missed. The areas of work of the two were similar – in fact, they were researching from the same starting-point – *but they themselves were different*. One was happy to have all the outside decisions made for him; the other was not. One left to work for the Government in an Organisation that was very Parental indeed; the other formed his own business, was bought out, and now runs his own company inside a multinational. Both were excellent, but their motivations could not be ascribed to the same simple concept of Self-Actualisation. What is true for the highest intellects is certainly true for the rest of the human race.

Some people simply want to get on with the job, get paid and fulfil their lives according to personal choice. These people, with whom I have great sympathy, work to live, not live to work. For them the massive communications battery of consultation and open management is a bore. Life is somewhere else, but they are perfectly willing to do a good and perhaps outstanding day's work. There is another class who live to be among the people at work: they use work as a vehicle for fulfilling their basic needs for human contact and, provided the work is reasonable, it is judged only on how it fulfils their contact needs.

Consultation in many large companies of the 70s became an

industry in itself. Joint consultative committees grew until something had to give. I know of one major company that used one of its most skilled managers on full-time consultation alone, and whose 'open door' policy increased the personal stress of many of its managers and their families to intolerable levels. However, the outstanding managers did set limits and provided the way forward from the extravagances. On the other hand, a Chairman of Unilever, before he rose to supreme office, told all new entrants that he was always available to arbitrate should there be a dispute with a superior. At the end of the arbitration one protagonist would leave the company. The clarity of the wording reduced the number of disputes miraculously. The Managing Director of a Middle Eastern oil company had an open door between certain hours, and a deputy for the rest. Semi-formal and scheduled briefing meetings replaced the chatter, and the real and measurable benefits rose.

Crude application of 'consultation is good' policies produces certain universal problems, the most important of which is that it provides an absolute limit to the size of organisations. If everyone is to be heard, then to reduce the noise to an acceptable level the numbers comprising 'everyone' must be limited. Five hundred souls seems to be the magical maximum for good work to happen without being swamped by the confused babble of communication. Secondly, and this time more importantly for the New Manager, time has to be given to thinking. Open doors are fine but, as we found in an earlier chapter, consultative management is not the only style, and certainly not the only appropriate style. It is also not the most effective style for many very effective managers. Open doors are fine until you want to think. The balance of personal survival and organisational structure has not, in my view, been struck; and so the New Manager needs to know a little more about the way organisations are being structured around him or her before we continue.

If Consultation is not the universal panacea, then maybe we ought to look at the detail of John Bloggs' problems. First, he explains quite clearly why the Parent – and in this case Nurturing Parent – organisation has failed. He sees both *endogenous* and *exogenous* factors. Coming from outside, he sees that the motivating tools of the Nurturing Parent organisation are losing their sharpness. Increasing affluence has led to the desire for personal choice in recreation, and while cricket and football can easily be provided by a single company, the whole range of the affluent society's leisure pursuits cannot.

The quality of outside provision has also risen. When Lord Leverhulme built his village, it contained an open-air swimming pool and a library, just as did Grandfather Bloggs'. When the County provided a sports centre with an Olympic pool, the most sensible line was taken. Unilever closed its own admirable little bath and donated money to improve the sports centre. Similarly the new public library virtually reduced the Lever library to an archive. The Parent organisation provides facilities with a view to structuring groups, and if affluence provides choice, the groups and the purpose for the facilities vanish. I met an acute example in a company Christmas dance. Over the years, tastes had changed and each sub-group wanted something different. The joint consultation committee took a vote and it was decided to run a theatre visit, a disco, a dinner dance and a boat trip. All were possible on the budget, and were allowed for one year. The next year the company attempted to revert to the Christmas dance: it was not supported and the function dissolved into local office parties in pubs.

In addition, from the outside have come the buffeting of the waves from competitors, changes in technology, changes in fashion, changes in government, changes in . . . Nothing is the same, and the Parent organisation is not equipped to react quickly. The Parent organisation relies on communication downward, communication from those at the helm to those in the engine room and on the decks. There is no tradition of the engine room communicating back that everyone else has converted from steam to diesel, let alone to diesel electric. There is no ready mechanism for the deck-hands to tell the helm about possible icebergs. The helm now needs the information desperately, and ways must be found of allowing the deck and the engine room to provide the information. Hence, the new drives towards the communicating organisation, with all its problems and side effects.

Internal factors, too, have reduced the effectiveness of the Nurturing Parent organisation. The other side of the contract of loyalty to the firm is the expectation of a job for life, and of a place for sons and daughters to work when they need it. The Nurturing Parent organisations loved families on their books:

> 'You must be Henry's little girl. I hope you give us as good service as your father – he is a wonderful worker.'

Redundancy stopped much of that, and in the UK what it did not stop was destroyed by reductions in juvenile recruitment. Henry may find himself attempting to keep himself working with the knowledge that his efforts will stop youngsters, including his own daughter, being recruited. The relationship of the worker to the organisation is never likely to be the same again.

Perhaps the simplest and least disruptive response to the weaknesses in the Nurturing Parent organisation could be called the *Little Professor organisation*. I would see the styles of management described in a range of books, including the 'Excellence' series of Peters and Peters, and Waterman and Blanchard's 'One Minute' series, as belonging to the Little Professor organisation. The Little Professor was described in Chapter 3, and the reader may remember it as an intermediate and creative form of the Child Ego state. The Little Professor works out all the angles, and acts in what is possibly seen from the outsider as an appropriate way, but in fact it is still operating from the totally egocentric Child state. The Little Professor organisation does exactly the same. Unlike the crude Consultative organisation, and indeed both of the Parent organisations, the Little Professor organisation works to no clear rules beyond pragmatism. If you were to question a sample of workers in a Little Professor organisation about the current organisational style, you would get a mixture of views. Some would see clear and firm leadership and control from the top, and claim Critical Parent control. Others would see consultation, even about the workplace itself, and believe they worked for a Consultative organisation. Others again would point to instances of the 'Hello Dolly' style of management and other symbols of the Nurturing Parent organisation, and they would be right, too. In the Little Professor organisation, there is no attempt to run away from the concept of strong management: the manager's job is to manage, but it is also to motivate and communicate.

First, the Little Professor organisation lays down clear and easily understood objectives, the principle being that of developing the organisation almost as a nation state, but in which the citizens have the right to decide that they do not like the flag. If Peters and Waterman were consulted by Mr John Bloggs, they might well ask him to look hard at his centre of excellence – at what his company did to distinguish itself from the others in the market-place. They would be asking Bloggs a question that he might find difficult. However, let us suppose that John decides that his company represents *quality* towards a small but regular set of commercial customers. Bloggs PLC sell to other markets, and sometimes sell on price and value for money, but Bloggs PLC is seen primarily as a company that supplies reliable, well-designed and well-built products commanding a premium price – Bloggs Make Well – Bloggs Components Never Let Your Customers Down. 'Right, ladies and gentlemen of the Bloggs empire,' John Bloggs would say, 'I may not be able to supervise you in detail, but this is a set of values within which you can operate without me breathing down your neck. Quality is the motto on our flag, and if any of you do *not wish* to take the personal consequences of working for an organisation with a flag of that colour, then leave now. If you would prefer to work at the volume end of the business, this is not your organisation and Goodbye.' Mr Bloggs would then explain something that Peters and Waterman would call 'Loose Tight Management' – as long as the managers and workers honour the flag of quality, they can have a very considerable measure of freedom. They have pre-ordained authority to sustain the quality of Bloggs products at all times, and with a very high measure of personal discretion. If, however, they wish to challenge the quality concept, they are fired. Bloggs can thereby maintain the organisation with an almost nationalist fervour.

Bloggs has defined his cutomer base, and so is able to 'get close to the customer' and understand his or her every need, within the context of quality. Bloggs knows the image the organisation is projecting, and he can therefore reward everyone in the organisation who conforms to that image. Bloggs will arrange rallies involving droves of his workers and make sure that 'everyone gets a prize'. We might well be invited to one of the regular 'get-togethers' where whole groups of workers are given badges for having achieved a certain reject rate or met to a particular safety target. The rates and targets will be set so that virtually 'everyone gets a prize', in the belief that everyone likes to get a prize and that it is more efficient to penalise the very bad than to make a problem out of the very special – and out of the people who are jealous of those whom the organisation has signalled as being very special.

Peters and Waterman might also advise a very 'loose tight' attitude to communication. Bloggs managers would be instructed to go out into the market-place. They would be told to work with their customers, in this case in their factories. They would also be told to meet with their staff and workers. The central administrative organisation would be cut to the bone, but the line managers would be told to 'manage by walking about'. Old Mr Bloggs J.P. would be amazed to find his grandson out on the shop floor for a significant part of his week. He might even be tempted to remember that that was how he started his business, and how the cares and complexities forced him to stay in his office. By walking about, Bloggs can begin to get over the rather sad little comment in his letter to us:

'Knowing what some of them do is also a problem.'

The newly trained Bloggs, perhaps inspired by Andrew S. Grove, late of the high technology organisation Intel, will find that he begins to trust the men and women working for him, even if the details of their technology is hidden. Talking to the gross specialist has the same motivational content as the concepts of his father's 'Hello Dolly' form of supervision. This time it is applied throughout the organisation, not simply to the shop floor.

I was asked to look at training issues in a company known to be a leader in high technology. The image from a visit to the factory that will persist in my mind is that of a silicon chip designer in his palace. The palace – a room bedecked with the modern crown jewels of high technology – multicoloured graphic representations contained a single man sitting at a console. He was very thin and looked exactly as I would imagine Mozart. My guide stood behind his back and introduced me to the palace: 'This is the veritable heart of our operation, and we are certainly looking at many hundreds of thousands of pounds of equipment. Of course, it's too complicated for any of us to understand. We get about five years at a maximum from these people. After that, we are not too certain.' And he went to leave. The young man did not react in any way until I asked him whether it was possible to zoom into one of the representations of a chip he was working on. He was very kind at first, and then began to radiate enthusiasm. It felt very good for both of us.

Grove and Peters and Waterman would certainly advise John Bloggs very strongly against managers having such attitudes to any of their staff. They would refuse managers permission to distance themselves from any valuable staff. They would also advise strongly against the conditions that caused another situation in another factory.

The organisation made products in sterile rooms. The products, designed for the veterinary market, were decanted from a range of large bottles, and the contents aseptically poured into ampules. The process, with its two workers in sterile clothing, was spectacular, and the room became part of the tourist circuit of the factory: visitors peered through the glass observation wall. The last group of visitors got more than they expected when one of the operatives looked round, made a monkey-like gesture and threw the contents of a full reagent bottle on the floor.

The principle of 'managing by walking about' is actually about communication and motivation. The Critical Parent organisation would see nothing wrong with 'showing visitors round' as if the workers were in a zoo. In practice, the world has changed and workers do matter, not just in abstract theory or out of wet liberalism, but in hard financial terms. Alienating the chip designer or the sterile-room worker costs real money, and the Little Professor organisation understands.

Bloggs will also be told that he has to communicate downwards to his workforce. The Little Professor organisation knows that bad news travels fast by itself, but that good news needs a messenger. Involving the workforce is essential if we are to have any chance, and good news is inclined to travel slower than bad.

The question must, then, be asked – Is genuine management possible with the Adult in charge, or are we stuck with the Parent and the Little Professor organisations for ever? The beginning of an answer lies, I believe, in the formation of the Informal Work-group. The stages of group formation happen: Joining and Belonging is followed by Role and Control and then Pairing and Sharing. The Parent organisations spend a great deal of effort encouraging the Joining and Belonging stage, but side-step the Role and Control issues by imposing roles and controls:

'I'm in charge and you are not.'

The side-stepping of the Role and Control issues *for the sake of the immediate task* does not make them go away. The group still needs its hierarchy and its roles, but they are necessarily outside the work pattern – we have the Queen Bee of the packing department and the resident clown, the top table in the canteen is reserved for particular ruling factions and a whole new hierarchy comes with union representations. The Pairing and Sharing phase happens after these issues have been solved. The group life runs parallel to the work life, which is still biased towards dealing with individuals in most organisations.

The Japanese import of Quality Circles goes some way towards allowing the Role and Control issues to be part of the work life. Existing work groups are encouraged, under their existing managers, to solve work problems. New teams are formed to look into issues and to report directly to the relevant top management. As the teams form, they need to explore new roles and new internal structures: some will be good at observation and others good at presentation, whilst others still may be good at analysis. The Quality Circle is designed to use people who want to be involved, and at its best it does not pressurise the individual who really does want to leave his or her 'brain on the hatstand' at work.

As I write, more techniques for running the workplaces of the future are being developed, and these will have their fanatical followers. The one certain thing is that they will bring new stresses on managers and workforces. The next chapter is intended to explain the issues raised by forced change, and to provide some sort of survival pack for the manager involved.

CHAPTER ELEVEN

The New Manager Takes A Grip on Things: Managing Change

'It happens so fast – you are just getting in touch with the last reorganisation when the next one comes.'

'Problems come from two sides: individuals crack up and the whole team reacts pretty oddly – it's as if I don't know them.'

'Not everyone reacts the same way. You tell them they are redundant: some say 'Yippee!', others collapse.'

'The cleaners know more than I do, and I'm management.'

'How do you manage change when you are as much concerned as the rest?'

Nothing in the world of management today is static. This chapter is designed to help the New Manager remain proactive in a world that encourages immobility in the individual. 'If you can keep your head when all about you are losing theirs and blaming you . . .', then you can truly claim to be a Good Manager. The changes around you will condense every management problem and bring them screaming to your door. I hope to share the problems of change and enable you to understand that certain stages in the development of individuals and organisations are inevitable, however painful; but that your effective survival and growth are not inevitable, though a little more likely with understanding.

> There is nothing more difficult to take in hand, more perilous to conduct, more uncertain in its success, than to take the lead in the introduction of a new order of things, because the innovator has for enemies all those who have done well under the old conditions, and lukewarm support in those who may do well under the new.
> Machiavelli (1446-1507), *The Prince*

The world of Change

The Bloggs company survived through all its changes but, as you will certainly have understood, gave its managers a very rough ride. When Mr J. Bloggs J.P. founded the company, he was working in fairly *placid* waters. The market could take pretty well everything he could make, provided that he was efficient and not too greedy. By the time plain J. Bloggs had become Sir John, things were different and competition was beginning to take hold. We can imagine Sir John meeting some of the other pillars of his industry and making deals, establishing trade associations or perhaps – perish the thought – *cartels*. Sir John, along with the William Hesketh Levers of this world, found that by establishing a near-*feudal* system of moats and drawbridges and agreements with the other barons, life could remain sweet. It did not remain sweet and, as Bloggs' organisation faced foreign competition – faced people who did not make deals – he employed the analysts, the *Operational Research* experts and the mathematicians to complete 'sensitivity analysis' for each and every area of his operations. Computers now, perhaps as the abacus had done earlier, would reign supreme, and linear programs would control all his factories, extracting the last squeak of profit from his established businesses. But suddenly, we can imagine, the computer and the experts began to fail Bloggs and his grandchildren.

During the first Arab–Israeli war a major company employed an economist to advise on the future of petro-chemicals – a major raw material for their business. Several weeks into the conflict, the economist was called to the board:

'At what price a barrel do you cease to be an expert?'

'That's a good question – at about $10, I would think.'

The next day the price of oil went to $13 a barrel and the expert was sacked. The same company employed an operations research specialist to predict the future of R & D organisations in the world. The expert looked at some five major factors, all of which could affect the future in question, and developed some ten different scenarios. The scenarios ranged from 'close everything' to the 'future is bright': together they presented an academically interesting but commercially useless portfolio. What had happened was that this company had arrived in *turbulent* water and the tools of logic and analysis no longer applied. In turbulent times, planning has its place; but survival, let alone progress, depends on the correct interventions of talented individuals.

The following stages will exist, given time, for all organisations:

> Placid
> Feudal
> Operations Research
> Turbulent

but industries vary in the rate at which they pass through the stages. Thus, the computer industry has moved through all the phases since 1946, whereas the foundry business has taken from the Hittites to the present to complete the set. Moreover, an industry does not necessarily survive as it attempts to change – the British Motor Cycle industry did not, and neither did the American Television industry.

Whatever your industry may be, the rate of change is increasing; and this increase pressurises and stresses both individuals and managers. Organisations are about inertia; they are designed to preserve working teams from the winds of change. They are cocoons which allow the work to proceed while the essentials are held. No production team will function effectively if it has to worry all the time about the rent, the heating bills and the pay slips, so we create Administration and Personnel. Organisations *are* inertia; they are the flywheels that smooth out the essential motions of the pistons.

The inertia of any organisation can be split into:

> Shared Values
> Mutual Self-Interest
> Controls

When one of the three is reduced, the others need to be brought up to compensate: otherwise the flywheel will cease to be of value, and the vibration of the piston will shake the organisation to pieces.

Yellow Trust is a charity working with underprivileged children in the towns of the industrial revolution. It provided food and shelter for thousands of children throughout the late nineteenth century, and has continued to do so up to the present day. Its founders were nonconformist Christians, and many of its workers have been part-time, working from their own church bases in their own communities very much in their own time, and receiving almost nominal salaries. The managers of the Trust responded to the national call for work in the new inner cities with their ethnic problems, and joined several other charities under a collective flag. The Trust very nearly fell apart.

If we look at the inertias of the Trust we will find very little *Control*. People have worked for the Trust because they shared its *values*, and had the job organised according to a Mutual Self-Interest. Working for the Trust was a worthy cause and, as non-conformist Christians, they grew in status within their own communities by working within sight of their own company of peers. The new values of a multi-ethnic society were not shared, and the loss of identity necessary to obtain the Government funding completed the loss of the Mutual Self-Interest factor for many of them. Because they were working for a pittance, the Control factors were simply non-existent. The part-time, old-established staff left, and the organisation nearly collapsed. The new organisation established a much tighter Control structure, employing full-time staff only, and recruited from the socially aware, regardless of creed. The new shared Values were humanistic, and to the Mutual Self-Interest, which previously had been devoted to the fulfilment of human contact needs, were now added the professional gains of money, use of an organisation car and influence in a wider community.

We can extend our metaphor of the flywheel and the vibration of the pistons. In a Placid environment, the vibration is unlikely to be great. The workforce has a clear task and is unlikely to be discontented. At the next – Feudal – stage, the workforce is likely to get organised and the organisational 'pistons' may start to become noisy. The use of Operations Research in itself is likely to increase internal pressures, but it is a very adequate flywheel that can smooth the turbulence of the final stage of an organisation.

EXERCISE

Look at your own organisation and attempt to see what are the inertias that keep it together.

What are your shared Values?
Do you believe in the mission of your organisation?
Do you find yourself able to make decisions in the knowledge that your values are the same as the organisation's?

What are your Mutual Self-Interests?
If you left the job now, what would you miss (security, a pension, friends, convivial workplace regular hours, challenges, organisation . . .)?
How much Control is necessary for you and your people to work effectively?
Is a time clock, in any form, necessary?
Disregarding the occasional difficult employee, is discipline a significant part of your job?

The early Parent organisations worked through Control mechanisms to establish stability. The new organisations, by attempting to agree on common Values, are attempting to move towards trust. To what extent has your organisation become a trusting organisation?

———————————▶

Just as organisations attempt to establish stability in their working lives, so do individuals – the extent depending on the individual. Freud saw the balance of excitement and change against stability as an important choice for our dignity. He saw it as a battle between two gods – Eros and Thanatos – and the personal choice in fixing our degree of subservience to each of the gods as being vital to us as human beings. When we have a particular difficulty – an Eros-dominated day at work – then we may well want a stable – Thanatos-dominated – evening in front of the television as a balance. How much stability each individual needs is a very personal thing and relates to the whole person. The balance between stability and its opposite is upset by any change, particularly when the change is forced upon us.

Imagine Joan has taken on the job of section head, Customer Services. On her first day, everything is new and she realises that a lot of her lifestyle will have to adapt. In her old job, she had been able to go shopping with her mother on Thursday evening, but now the review meeting is that day and she will have to work late: Friday evening is more crowded in the supermarket, but 'needs must'. The office has a No Smoking Area and her desk is in the middle, but she was trying to give up anyway. Lots of little things that she will have to change . . .

After a few weeks she has decided that it would be more convenient if her desk were out of the main office, so that she would not have to worry about smoking – if she wanted to, that is. The

Friday shopping is still a nuisance, but otherwise things are going well, with a little bit of give and take. Luckily there is less 'give' these days, now that she is settling in.

Towards the beginning of the first year, Joan has decided that the Thursday meeting is not the way she wants to run the department. A written report from all her staff to a proforma works well, and she can review everybody's on Thursday afternoon. Her mother did not really like the crowded Friday supermarket.

Joan began by adapting herself to the new job, but then gradually adapted the job to her: this we all do to a greater or lesser extent.

Problems arise when we stay in a personalised job for too long, and lose the ability to adapt . . .

Suppose Joan is now well established and her balance of excitement to regularity is settled, with a strong emphasis on regularity. You are Joan's manager and, along with two other supervisors, this is your world: Joan, Customer Services; Harry, Factory Quality Control; and Peter, Stores and Goods Input Check.

The company is in financial trouble and, although various minor cuts in your three departments have worked in the past, you are unhappy that further, more drastic, efforts may be required. The axe falls when you are called to attend a senior planning meeting and you are told that your three sections will have to become two, involving various redundancy plans to produce a 25 per cent cut by the end of the year in six months' time. 'We would be grateful for a detailed report on your proposals to implement these decisions by Friday.' You leave feeling squashed, a feeling compounded by your car not being ready at the garage.

Going home in the works bus, you meet Joan – it is her section that you feel most able to cut. You feel that by bringing together Factory Quality Control and Customer Services there might be the necessary savings . . . Joan is a meticulous, careful and perhaps dull worker and, having read this book, you know her as a Logic, interested in the four Ws of What, Where, When and Who. You do not mention your thoughts on reorganisation, but do ask her advice on possible efficiency improvements – after all, she guards her section like 'a tiger with her cubs', and you do not really know what goes on. Joan is very positive indeed, and promises to give you her ideas in writing. In the morning you have made up your mind to chop Joan's section – just as her report, the result of much burning of midnight oil on her part, arrives on your desk. It is full of sound sense, and in a world of less drastic remedies it would certainly be worth considering.

You thank Joan but go ahead with your plan, using some of Joan's ideas for the new combined section. Joan is redeployed, but many of her staff are made redundant. How does Joan feel? What is likely to happen? Has your handling of the incident made the situation any worse?

Let's look at the respective diagrams for Joan's and your adapation to change:

In the bus

YOU   JOAN

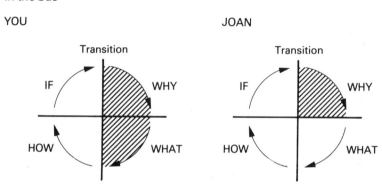

In the morning

YOU   JOAN

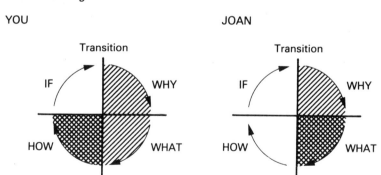

While you are in your *How* Phase – *how* to implement the decision
you have you have already made – Joan is in her *What* phase,
collecting data. The very fact that you are out of phase will make
things much worse. Having made a decision, you do not wish to be
challenged and are likely, at best, to feel you need to defend
yourself and justify your recommendations. Joan is still trying to
be helpful and your defence will confuse her. If, however, you do
not defend, but go into the attack in order to justify yourself, then
Joan may be really hurt.

——————▶

EXERCISE

> What happens when any of us has a change forced upon us?
> Imagine a recent change that has been forced on you against
> your instinctive wishes. The change may have been an 'Act of
> God', an accident, or one produced by specific persons whom
> you can name.
>
> Think of the actual time and place you heard of the change, and
> how the information came to you.
>   How did you feel before the change, and how did you feel
> immediately after you had heard? How did you feel towards the
> change-bearer, if there was one?
>
> Push yourself forward in time.
> How did you feel when the change had sunk in, and how do you
> feel now?
>
> Write down the emotions that you felt, at first and on
> reflection.

——————▶

I have had a great number of emotions suggested by managers
and, without knowing the changes they were recording, I remain
intrigued. However, the point that is likely to issue from your list,
and from every such list, is that forced change produces some
pretty unpleasant feelings in all of us. We prefer to plan our own
changes, and to take them at our own pace.
     Using the learning cycle, we can arrange the emotions in a
logical order. Change produces a sequence of responses,
beginning with *Shock*, followed by *Defence/Retreat* when we try
to pretend it didn't happen, *Acknowledgement* when regretfully
we accept it has, and finally *Acceptance* when we make the best of
it. These correspond nicely to the cycle of *Why*, *What*, *How* and *If*
stages.

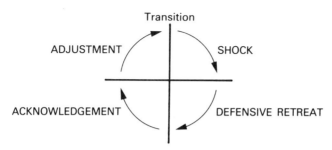

Alternatively, open up the circle, put in some of the words I have found managers use to explain their reaction to enforced change, and we have the following:

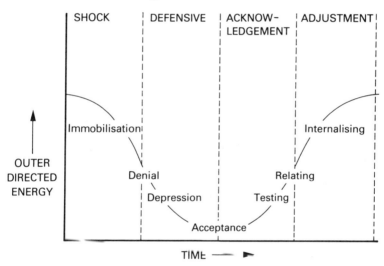

When we undergo a change, we can pass through all the emotions I have listed. If the change is small, or welcome, or we feel particularly good about ourselves before the transition, then the trough can be very shallow and the energy available to enable us to face the world can remain high. On the other hand, if the change is large and novel and unwelcome, or if we are already feeling low, then the energy available to help us get on with our life can become very low indeed. There is also no guarantee that we will complete the cycle or come out of the valley. We may stop anywhere in the cycle, and the emotions that might be missed in transit will become magnified by our thinking about them:

'There is nothing good or bad but thinking makes it so.'

Lose a few nights' sleep and do your thinking between two and four in the morning, and changes that you would normally take in your stride become icebergs of Titanic proportions.

Let's go back to Joan and the moment that she heard her section was to be disbanded and she herself redeployed. Being a *What* person, she probably moved pretty rapidly into her sector of analysis, disregarding the *Why* questions. Joan would be most vulnerable in relation to *How* to survive the changes. I could see her getting very depressed, and perhaps angry, but unable to relate her analysis to real life. Working with Joan, we would have to help her make choices from the carefully structured alternatives she had developed.

Using the descriptions of Chapter 8, you may be able to see the particular traps the other three personality groups set for themselves and how, as a manager, you might be called upon to help. The *Why* people may well 'seek hidden meanings' and become bemused. They need facts and clarity so that they can structure their problems into the next sector of the cycle. The *What* people have already been discussed, but the *How* people have moved on and obtained a set of decisions on what they *ought* to do. Unfortunately, the *oughts* that come from their Critical Parent are inclined not to happen, and we need to give them guidance and permission to try their solutions in real life. The *How* person can easily move into helplessness and despair without such help. The *If* people – to make a gross generalisation – either need no help at all (they have realised the hidden opportunities of the change and grasped them) or they present us with the greatest challenges. The *If* Enthusiasts will have taken the chance – spent the redundancy money on a small business or a new car – and may have done the wrong thing.

EXERCISE

Look at the table overleaf and relate it to individuals you know. What sort of behaviours did you notice when they reacted to a particular forced change?
If you had been a manager or friend at the time, what help could you have given?

Imagine a major change in a whole organisation.
What would you expect to happen if a large number of people all received bad news about their jobs at the same time?

How would you as a manager expect to have to react?

How would your own feelings and emotions influence what you could actually do?

Stages of the individual during change

Stage	Feelings	Perception	Emotions	Structure
Shock	Threat to what you know	Being overwhelmed	Panic, helplessness	Confusion
Defence/ Retreat	Holding to to the old way	Avoidance – wishful-thinking	Indifference, anger, euphoria	Defences
Acknow-ledgement	Giving up the old/self doubt	Facing reality	Depression, bitterness	Dis-/re-organisation
Adjust-ment	New self-worth	New reality-testing	Gradual growth in satisfaction	Rebuilding

The managing of a major change calls for a level of management flexibility that is very often beyond the skills of one person. However, if you have never learnt to use what I called earlier the 'Management Helicopter', you are making it very hard for yourself. Managing change does need the 'overall view' and, if you are totally open and known by your staff, such a view with its implication of appropriate toughness – is impossible. People in change need to establish their own dignity, and very often that means turning their backs on you. The high Nurturing Parents, the high Joining and Belongers, the weak Shapers and strong Team Workers and the dominant *Why* and *What* managers – these will be particularly vulnerable.

Ken ran a small co-operative supermarket in his own district, and prided himself on knowing all his customers on first-name terms. He had certainly developed the job to suit his style, and his style was to be everywhere and know every job. If the checkout was pressed, he was on the till. If a stacker was sick, he was on the price-tagging machine.

It was his assistant's birthday and they had a party in the
storeroom which progressed into a local ex-serviceman's club.

'Heard that they are closing down the smaller branches – you won't
let it happen to *us*, Ken . . .?'

Ken said No, but found the letter that advised him of the branch
closure in the next day's post. He had a breakdown, and a manager
from Head Office had to arrange the redundancy payments and
transfers.

What happens when a number of people go through a major
change together? Well, the simple answer is that they don't – that
individuals react differently. On the other hand, organisations
do go through the stages of Shock, Defence/Retreat, Ac-
knowledgment and Adaptation in a recognisable way.

In the Shock phase, Ken's store was chaotic and nobody, except
one of the early morning cleaners, seemed to know what was going
on. There were a few rows between the storeman, who was usually
very timid, and the stackers, and nobody could be found to resolve
them. Ken's temporary successor, Mrs West, decided to delay her
arrival until some of the heat had gone out of the situation:

'I know what will need to be done in the next weeks and there is
no way I'm going to get involved in the petty struggles that will
resolve themselves once the inevitability of closure sinks in.'

Mrs West, arrived during the Defence/Retreat stage, almost at the
same time as the Regional Organiser of the Shop Workers Union.
She was surprised to meet the Union because up to then the branch
had remained the only one that was non-unionised in the group.
The storeman was now refusing to communicate directly with the
rest of the shop unless it was put in writing – 'he'll want it in
triplicate if he can find enough carbon paper,' was the comment
from one of the till girls, who was getting married anyway.

   Mrs West – whom readers of this book could recognise as having
some Shaper characteristics, and before reading this book might
have seen as an illegitimate daughter of Attila the Hun – called a
staff meeting. The staff went away subdued, but the shelves got
filled and the visit by the Health Inspector proved an anti-climax.

   About a month after Mrs West's arrival and two months before
the closure date, the store entered the Acknowledgement phase.
There was an amazing staff party for the checkout girl's wedding
which resulted in *all* members of the branch being banned for life
from the ex-servicemen's club. Mrs West surprised them all by

playing the piano and knowing some quite remarkable community songs. In the morning she was faced by the storeman, who accused her of destroying his authority. At the end of the meeting they had developed a method by which slow-moving stock could be 'borrowed' on a sale or return basis from a main branch. It was the first of many tough but useful discussions in which Mary West explored, with the staff, methods of softening the individual blows.

On the last day of the store, Mary was given a large bunch of flowers.

Managing forced change

Normally individuals will adapt to change at their own pace. The stages they go through are:

Shock
Defence/Retreat
Acknowledgement
Successful Adaptation

Problems arise because:

1. The pace is forced.
2. Individuals or groups are allowed to rest too long in an undisturbed state, and lose the ability to change; or when a change occurs, they are allowed to stay too long in one of the stages.
3. Local or central management fails to deal with the behaviour of groups or individuals concerned with the change.
4. The stages of change get out of phase for parts of the group or organisation – in the example of the supermarket, the stores might have adjusted but bizarre behaviour from the counter staff could well have made them revert.
5. The manager is not able to dissociate him- or herself from the process, and seeks to justify or blame.
6. Individuals cannot cope.

─────▶

EXERCISE

Consider an enforced change that your organisation has had to make recently.

Using the information you now have about yourself and others, how well was the change managed?

Would you, with hindsight, have done things differently?

Did any individuals find themselves unable to cope?

What would you now attempt that would have made the change more smooth, for yourself, the staff and the organisation?

───────►

CHAPTER TWELVE

Bringing It Together and Over to You

'When all is said and done, there is more said than done.'

It has been a long journey, and I feel we have attempted a great deal. I am not able to say, 'Its all in there . . . just turn to page x.' – life is not like that. Before I ask you to do what is *your last exercise*, let's review the ground.

We began by looking at the complexity of human communication, and by showing how written or telephone communication had traps and pitfalls. We then went on to look at a model of human personality produced by Eric Berne, which gave words to the various states of mind we can find ourselves acting from. We moved towards an understanding that the way we are perceived by others may well mask the way we are received by others. We also began to discuss differences in the way individuals react to change.

By Chapter 4 we were able to deal with the issue of motivation, and initially we looked at the way the New Manager may find him- or herself limited in what they are able to do to motivate their staff. I then introduced the concept of individuals needing human contact, and developed this theme in two ways: first, to show how we, together with our organisations, structure our demand for human contact; and secondly, to show how individuals and groups 'organise' their contact needs in a sequence – Joining and Belonging – Role and Control – Pairing and Sharing. We saw how a manager with a great urgency towards completing a task could easily be swamped by his or her group, settling in. I also discussed how the 'organisation' of contact needs determined the life cycle of a team, and gave advice on how a team could be brought artificially towards maturity through the definition of clear objectives and clear roles for its members. The process of clear goal-definition occupied the next pages, and this was followed by a somewhat detailed analysis of the roles required in effective teams. I showed that some of the so-called 'personality clashes' in our working groups are avoidable through a process of negotiation with others, so that we understand each other's contributions and do not step on each other's toes.

At this point, I felt it was reasonable to consider the job that you as a New Manager have undertaken, and attempted to demonstrate that the job has different perspectives. We looked at these perspectives in terms of what I called the *Why*, the *What*, the *How* and the *If* dominated managers. I suggested that organisations needed all of these personalities, but that it was not always easy for them to get on with each other.

Our next concerns were the organisations within which we have to function. We saw that the Parent-dominated organisations had largely been replaced by organisations attempting to use the whole employee – attempting to see people not merely as a set of skills or a cypher, but as sentient beings with creativity. We saw that the changes produced by the movements towards honouring the employee gave the manager new problems. These were covered in the final chapter, on managing change. I hope that by now you will understand that individuals and groups all pass through a series of gates in their adaptation to change, and that the skilled manager is able to help rather than hinder that progress.

---▶

EXERCISE – NOW IT'S UP TO YOU

Drawing on my experience of working with managers, I would say that if you, the New Manager beginning your journey, have found three or four points in this book that have caught your eye, and which you think are appropriate to you – that's great! The problem is that, to make the exercise worthwhile, we have to use such information. We have to test it in our actual world, to see if it has the germ of something that will help us.

Look at what you wrote in response to the first two exercises in Chapter 1. The first one was concerned with Blocks and Barriers and the second with your learning objectives.

1. Write down, on separate pieces of paper, not fewer than three or more than six points of interest that you have gathered from the book.

2. How, looking at each of these points in turn, would their application improve your efficiency as a manager?

3. What precisely would be your objective in the application, and how would you measure the improvement in your efficiency?

4. Look at all the points to see if there are any conflicting factors.

5. Identify the factors that will assist you in the achievement of your objectives:
   (a) in others (the organisation, your staff . . .);
   (b) in yourself.

6. Identify the factors that will oppose you in the achievement of your objectives:
   (a) in others;
   (b) in yourself.

7. How can you increase and strengthen the positive factors and reduce the negatives; and who else needs to know what you are doing?

8. Review and decide whether what you have considered is:
   (a) theoretically realistic;
   (b) something you actually want to do and will do.

If the answers to 8a and 8b are both Yes, then do it!

⎯⎯⎯⎯⎯⎯▶